KU-019-136

BLACK POPPIES

BRITAIN'S BLACK COMMUNITY AND THE GREAT WAR

STEPHEN BOURNE

The History Press

This book is dedicated to my sister, Linda Bourne Hull

First published 2014

The History Press
The Mill, Brimscombe Port
Stroud, Gloucestershire, GL5 2QG
www.thehistorypress.co.uk

© Stephen Bourne, 2014

The right of Stephen Bourne to be identified as the Author
of this work has been asserted in accordance with the
Copyright, Designs and Patents Act 1988.

All rights reserved. No part of this book may be reprinted
or reproduced or utilised in any form or by any electronic,
mechanical or other means, now known or hereafter invented,
including photocopying and recording, or in any information
storage or retrieval system, without the permission in writing
from the Publishers.

British Library Cataloguing in Publication Data.
A catalogue record for this book is available from the British Library.

ISBN 978 0 7524 9760 0

Typesetting and origination by The History Press
Printed in Great Britain

CUMBRIA LIBRARIES

3 8003 04504 1175

County Council

Libraries, books and more . . .

BARROW LIBRARY		
9114 RESERVE STOCK 4|16		

Please return/renew this item by the last due date.
Library items may be renewed by phone on
030 33 33 1234 (24 hours) or via our website
www.cumbria.gov.uk/libraries

Cumbria Libraries
CLIC
Interactive Catalogue

Ask for a CLIC password

CONTENTS

ACKNOWLEDGEMENTS

The Authors' Foundation
Black and Asian Studies Association
Black Cultural Archives
British Film Institute (www.bfi.org.uk)
British Library (www.bl.uk)
Commonwealth War Graves Commission (www.cwgc.org)
Eastside Community Heritage
Imperial War Museum (London) (www.iwm.org.uk)
London Borough of Southwark Libraries
London Borough of Southwark Local History Library
National Archives
West Indian Ex-Services Association
Suzanne Bardgett, Imperial War Museum, London
Terry Bolas
Kevin Brownlow
Sean Creighton
Kim Cooper, Principal Library Officer, Cornish Studies Library
Ray Costello, historian
Peter Devitt, Assistant Curator, RAF Museum, London
Audrey Dewjee
Robert Fleming, Curator (Access & Outreach), National Army Museum,
    London
Jeffrey Green (www.jeffreygreen.co.uk)

David Hankin (www.davidhankin.com)
Tina Horsley
Keith Howes
Molly Hull
Stephen Humphrey
Howard Rye
Marika Sherwood, Senior Researcher, Institute of Commonwealth Studies
Dr Richard Smith, Goldsmiths University of London
Helena Stride, Imperial War Museum, London
The staff (Meno Jacob, Fred Haynes, Jessica Nyantakyi and Sandria Cruise) of Brandon Library, Walworth, London SE17
Thanks to Mrs Anita Bowes and the Cozier family for permission to reproduce their copy of the photo of Pastor Kamal Chunchie and the Coloured Men's Institute outing to Reigate (1926). Pastor Chunchie's copy of this photo can be found in the archive of Eastside Community Heritage, The Old Town Hall, Stratford, London E15 4BQ, courtesy of his family.

AUTHOR'S NOTE

In *Black Poppies* the terms 'black' and 'African Caribbean' refer to Caribbean and British people of African origin. Other terms, such as 'West Indian', 'negro' and 'coloured' are used in their historical contexts, usually before the 1960s and 1970s, the decades in which the term 'black' came into acceptable use.

My feeling, always, has been that although the combatants (and to some extent those who aid them directly on the battlefield and theatres of war) are in the line of fire throughout their active service, 'war' also involves and impacts on specific communities far from the front, as well as the citizens of all the countries embroiled in the conflict: physically, psychologically and spiritually. *Black Poppies* reflects this view.

In spite of its title, *Black Poppies* is not intended to be a book specifically about black servicemen in the First World War. The book intends to highlight some of the experiences of black servicemen *and* the wider black community in Britain from 1914 to 1919. To achieve this aim, *Black Poppies* has been divided into three main sections. Part I focuses on the experiences of black servicemen including individuals such as Walter Tull and regiments such as the British West Indies Regiment. Part II highlights the lives of some black citizens who lived in Britain through the First World War and Part III explores the impact of the 1919 anti-black riots on three black communities in Britain: those in London, Cardiff and Liverpool. The final chapter, 'Black Britain, 1919', surveys what else was happening in Britain's black community just after the end of the war, and includes references to some of the political organisations that were being established at that time.

Black Poppies should not be read in isolation. An early publication worth reading is Sir Harry H. Johnston's *The Black Man's Part in the War* (1917). Johnston told how commanders had praised black troops for their 'pluck, gallantry and devotion', and for the tenacity with which they stood up to heavy machine-gun fire. Since Peter Fryer's landmark book *Staying Power: The History of Black People in Britain* was published in 1984, several important books have surfaced that include vital information about the lives of black servicemen and Britain's black community during the First World War. Some of these are now out of print, but I would suggest that readers access them through inter-library loans, the British Library, eBay, or a second-hand book dealer such as www.abebooks.co.uk. I would highly recommend the following: *Under the Imperial Carpet: Essays in Black History 1780–1950* (1986), edited by Rainer Lotz and Ian Pegg, which includes chapters about black soldiers in the army in the First World War (by David Killingray) and the 1919 riots (by Jacqueline Jenkinson); Jeffrey Green's *Black Edwardians: Black People in Britain 1901–1914* (1998) for its detailed survey of the black presence in Britain in the period leading upto the outbreak of the First World War; Ray Costello's *Black Liverpool: The Early History of Britain's Oldest Black Community 1730–1918* (2001) for its study of the oldest established black community in one of Britain's leading sea ports; Glenford Howe's *Race, War and Nationalism: A Social History of West Indians in the First World War* (2002) for its analysis of the impact of the First World War on the people of the Caribbean and Richard Smith's *Jamaican Volunteers in the First World War: Race, Masculinity and the Development of National Consciousness* (2004) for its analysis of the impact of the First World War on Jamaican recruits into the British Army and the British West Indies Regiment. More information about these books and other relevant texts can be found in the Further Reading list at the end of this book.

As a community historian, I have always tried to include first-hand testimonies in my black British history books. However, for *Black Poppies*, first-hand accounts have been almost impossible to find because so few black servicemen from the First World War have been interviewed. For example, in 1964 the BBC's ambitious and ground-breaking twenty-six-part series *The Great War* overlooked the contribution of African Caribbean servicemen and the British West Indies Regiment. For this reason I am indebted to the makers of the outstanding documentary film *Mutiny* (1999), written and researched by Tony T. and Rebecca

Goldstone at Sweet Patootee. This was shown on Channel 4. In his review of *Mutiny*, published in the journal *Caribbean Studies* (2008), Richard Smith noted that 'by deploying interview footage of three of the handful of West Indian First World War veterans still alive in the 1990s, *Mutiny* attempts to reclaim this forgotten history through the voices of the servicemen themselves, a tradition pioneered by the producers of *The Great War* series.' The revealing and illuminating interviews with the handful of surviving soldiers who served with the British West Indies Regiment include the Guyanese Gershom Browne (aged 101) and the Jamaican Eugent Clarke (aged 106). They vividly recalled their lives in the trenches on the front line.

First-hand testimony is also present in Ernest Marke's autobiography *Old Man Trouble* (1975) in which he presented a dramatic insight into his experiences as a young merchant seaman in the First World War. Norman Manley's short autobiography, published in *Jamaica Journal* (1973), in which he reflects in detail on his war service, has also been extremely useful, but it is heartbreaking that so few first-hand testimonies of black servicemen in the First World War have been recorded and preserved.

The same is also true of the black community in Britain during the First World War, though two landmark television programmes, *The Black Man in Britain 1550–1950* (BBC2, 1974) and Colin Prescod's *Tiger Bay is My Home* (Channel 4, 1983), have proved invaluable for their inclusion of first-hand accounts of the 1919 race riots in Cardiff.

My own work as a community historian included, in the late 1980s and early 1990s, a series of interviews with my adopted aunt, Esther Bruce, a mixed-race Londoner born in 1912. First-hand accounts of her early childhood, some of them previously unpublished, are reproduced in this book and they help to give an insight into the lives of Britain's black working-class people during the First World War. It was my relationship to Aunt Esther that inspired me to undertake further research into the lives of black Britons, as well as African and Caribbean settlers in the UK (see Introduction). This eventually led me to write books on the subject including two for The History Press: *Mother Country: Britain's Black Community on the Home Front 1939–45* (2010) and *The Motherland Calls: Britain's Black Servicemen and Women 1939–45* (2012). These two books include the stories of several black Britons who were born just before or during the First World War. In adulthood most of them took active roles in the Second World War and demonstrated their patriotism. They came from all walks of life and social classes, and as a group they offer a 'snapshot' of black British lives that must have been influenced by the First World War (most of them were children at the time).

In *Mother Country* I included Birmingham-born army sergeant Jack Artis (1918–98); Lambeth-born civilian defence worker Len Bradbrook (1904–91); West Hartlepool-born Ivor Cummings (1913–92), an Assistant Welfare Officer for the Colonial Office; Manchester-born civilian defence worker Len Johnson (1902–69); Plymouth-born civilian defence worker William 'Bill' Miller (1890–1970); Devon-born conscientious objector Basil Rodgers (1900–83); and the Chesire-born singer Ida Shepley (1908–75). In *The Motherland Calls* I included the Liverpool-born WAAF Lilian Bader (1918–) and her London-born husband Ramsay Bader (1919–92), who served in the army; London-born jazz composer and RAF intelligence officer Reginald Foresythe (1907–58); the London-born jazz musician and RAF flight sergeant and physical training instructor Ray Ellington (1915–85); the Yorkshire-born musician Geoff Love (1917–91); and the London-born army officer Charles 'Joe' Moody (1917–2009), the first black Briton to be commissioned since Walter Tull in the First World War.

Finally, more research needs to be undertaken for a fuller appreciation and understanding of the subject of *Black Poppies*. Financial constraints have made it impossible for me to pursue what David Killingray proposed in *Under the Imperial Carpet* in 1986, but I am hopeful that *Black Poppies* will inspire others to undertake further research as described by Killingray:

> A more detailed study of open papers at the Public Record Office [...] especially War Office and Colonial Officers papers, would probably reveal a fuller picture of black involvement in the Great War. Another fruitful source is likely to be the press, particularly British local newspapers and also the newspapers published in the Caribbean and West African colonies which invariably carried information about local men who had enlisted. But perhaps a more useful avenue of research is through the collection of a family and oral history from within the British black community, a task which can most profitably be undertaken by members of that community.

Though every care has been taken, if, through inadvertence or failure to trace the present owners, I have included any copyright material without acknowledgement or permission, I offer my apologies to all concerned.

INTRODUCTION

Every year, on 24 May, we celebrated Empire Day at school. All the girls wore white and all the boys wore their best suits. Half-way through the morning we were told to put our inks away and then we marched along North End Road waving our Union Jacks. Everybody stopped to watch us march. The head girl of the school was dressed as Britannia. We had to salute her. 'Rule Britannia!' Then we had half a day's holiday.

Esther Bruce (1912–94) (see Chapter 12)

Growing up in a culturally diverse part of London in the 1960s, I absorbed a lot of what was going on around me. I come from a working-class family and was raised on a housing estate in Peckham. From 1962 to 1969 I was a pupil in a racially mixed primary school on Peckham Road. My school included a new generation of children from African and Caribbean backgrounds: their parents had come to Britain as part of the large-scale post-Second World War migration of Commonwealth citizens. When I was a youngster, what British children of *all* cultural backgrounds were *not* made aware of – in schools, in history books, by the media, and only very rarely in films and on television – was that there had been a black presence in Britain since at least the mid-sixteenth century (see Chronology). Black historical figures from the past had been made invisible. Perhaps if this situation had been different, Britain's first large-scale generation of black children might have felt better equipped to deal with racism. Perhaps white children, and their parents, might have been less disposed towards racism if they had been adequately informed about the longstanding black presence within Britain's national story. The invisibility of, and silence around, Britain's black history (or, on a more personal level, black British histories) is, of course, a problem that permeates British society and culture to this day. I have lost count of the times I have read books about the two world wars and discovered that Britain's black and Asian citizens and other colonial subjects have been excluded.

Regarding my own awareness, I consider myself lucky. As a white child growing up in Britain, I had in my family an adopted aunt who had been born black and British long before the arrival of the ship the *Empire Windrush* at Tilbury docks on 22 June 1948. This marked the beginning of post-war settlement in Britain of people from Africa, Guyana and the Caribbean. *Windrush* carried the first wave of settlers who were seeking a new life in the land they called the 'Mother Country'. Unlike my contemporaries, my relationship to Aunt Esther (see Chapter 12), who had been born in London in 1912, just before the outbreak of the First World War, gave me, from an early age, an awareness of the pre-1948 black presence in Britain.

I did not view the post-war settlers as a 'threat', or agree with those who began suggesting that 'immigrants' be repatriated. I was an impressionable 10-year-old on 20 April 1968 when the Conservative MP Enoch Powell made his inflammatory and objectionable 'Rivers of Blood' speech on immigration from the Commonwealth. He said, 'we must be mad, literally mad, as a nation to be permitting the annual flow of 50,000 dependants [...] It is like watching a nation busily engaged in heaping up its own funeral pyre.' At the same time, in British homes up and down the country, his fictional disciple, Alf Garnett, shouted racist abuse in the BBC's situation comedy series *Till Death Us Do Part*. So it did not surprise me that, as a teenager in the 1970s, I witnessed a rise in popularity of the National Front, a far-right, whites-only political party. I will never forget the horror of watching – from my bedroom window – National Front supporters marching along Peckham Road with a police escort. It was like watching a Nazi rally in Germany in the 1930s. Clearly, growing up in a racially mixed community, and having an adopted aunt who was black and British, gave me insights that most white children in Britain did not get.

In 1974 I watched a fascinating television series on BBC2 called *The Black Man in Britain 1550–1950*. This was one of the first programmes on British television to document the history of black people in Britain over 400 years. From this series I learned about many black historical figures from Britain's past, including the Africans Ignatius Sancho (1729–80), a writer, and Olaudah Equiano (1745?–1797), an abolitionist. However, the episode that had the most impact on me was the one that featured interviews with elders from the black communities in Cardiff and Liverpool. These included Joe Friday (see Chapter 17) who recalled the terrifying anti-black race riots which occurred in a number of British seaports in 1919 in the aftermath of the First World War.

Meanwhile, older members of my family, including Aunt Esther, informed me about life on the home front in the Second World War: air raids, evacuation, food shortages, doodlebugs and how communities pulled together and tried to survive these terrible ordeals. However, very few of them had lived through or could remember the First World War. I did have two grandfathers who served in the First World War, but they never spoke about their experiences. For example, my mother's stepfather, Horace Dulieu, born in Peckham, London, in 1896, was sent to the battlefields of France in 1916 when he was just 19 years old. As children, my sister and I knew something terrible had happened to him because he was blinded in one eye, but we never asked him about it. He had only been in France for a few weeks when a German sniper shot him in the face. Grandad's face and eye were stitched on the battlefield and he was sent home. I shall never forget the distress caused to him when, in 1964, the BBC screened its acclaimed twenty-six-part documentary series *The Great War*. It brought back too many painful and traumatic memories for Grandad. However, in the thousands of books and television documentaries that have chronicled the First World War, at least the stories of men like my grandfather have been documented. This is not the case with servicemen who came from African and Caribbean backgrounds.

The near-total exclusion from our history books of black servicemen in the First World War is shameful. One of the few exceptions has been Walter Tull (1888–1918). In recent years he has become the most celebrated black British soldier of the First World War (see Chapter 2). Books and television documentaries have ensured Tull his place in British history but he did not exist in isolation. With the centenary of the First World War from 2014 to 2018, there are many others who have been overlooked in the history books and should be acknowledged, and *Black Poppies* will highlight some of those men. In addition to the servicemen,

Black Poppies will highlight the lives of some of the black and mixed-race population of Britain who were living in the country from 1914 to 1918. They were not necessarily involved in war work, but the book will attempt to give an *impression* or 'snapshots' of the lives of Britain's diverse black community at that time. Clearly there are equivalent histories to be written about the historical presence of Britain's Indian, Chinese and other immigrant communities in the First World War. My book is not intended to be a continuation of Jeffrey Green's informative book *Black Edwardians: Black People in Britain 1901–1914* (1998). However, Jeffrey has been a great support to me and a valuable source of information. I would highly recommend his book to readers and using it as a 'companion' to *Black Poppies*.

Regarding the role of black women serving the British during the First World War, very little information is available. As explained in Chapter 12, women of African descent from all social classes in Britain had very few employment options. They either went on the stage or took jobs as seamstresses. The Liverpool historian Ray Costello has shared some information about one of his aunts who was a seamstress and who made caps and uniforms in Liverpool's Lybro Factory during the war. He explained that the factory was owned by Quakers and was one of the few that would employ black women in Liverpool (see Chapter 3). More research needs to be undertaken to find out if any other black or mixed-race women were employed in war factories. As far as the nursing profession is concerned, there appears to have been a 'colour bar' until the Second World War. In the 1930s, Dr Harold Moody and his League of Coloured Peoples (see Chapter 19) campaigned for British hospitals to lift this barrier, and to train and employ black nurses, but so far no evidence has come to light that there were black or mixed-race women within the ranks of the British military nursing services, or the British Red Cross VADs. There may have been a few Anglo-Indian women somewhere, but assuming that these would have had British fathers and Indian or Anglo-Indian mothers, it has not been possible to identify them. When interviewed by the author in 2013, Sue Light, who has undertaken research into the role of women in the First World War and contributed to The Western Front Association's website, said:

> I know of no evidence of black women training as nurses within the UK at that time. There were black trained nurses in the USA during WW1, but those attached to the military were not allowed to proceed overseas to

Europe, and were restricted to working in hospitals for black soldiers. The one or two instances of black women applying to join Queen Alexandra's Imperial Military Nursing Service (QAIMNS) pre-war were also black Americans. So I can only say that I have never read about, or seen photos of, black nurses in the UK or with the British medical services overseas during WW1. There were probably Indian civilian women working in British hospitals in India in domestic roles, and also as local staff in places such as Egypt and Mesopotamia. There could always have been exceptions, and I would never say there were no black women nursing in the UK's civil hospitals, but I don't think it was ever the case in military hospitals. If there were black nurses in Europe at that time, I would think they were most likely to be American.

Some black servicemen made the ultimate sacrifice in the First World War and, like Walter Tull, died on the battlefields but, with the passage of time, with the exception of Tull, the contributions of black servicemen have been forgotten. It is hoped that *Black Poppies* and the centenary of the First World War will help to change that.

BLACK BRITAIN 1555–1919: A CHRONOLOGY

1555:	A group of five Africans, from what is now known as Ghana, visited England to be trained as interpreters for English merchants.
1558–1603:	During the reign of Elizabeth I, England began to participate in the transatlantic slave trade.
1562–63:	An unscrupulous adventurer, Sir John Hawkins, made the first English Atlantic slave voyage, acquiring at least 300 inhabitants of the Guinea coast.
1570–1807:	Some African slaves were brought to England to work as servants and entertainers, and there were African musicians and dancers at the court of Elizabeth I.
1596:	Elizabeth I issued a proclamation ordering the expulsion of black settlers from England.
1601:	Elizabeth I issued a second proclamation, ordering the Lord Mayor of London to expel all 'negroes and blackamoors' from London.
1698–1720:	London became the leading slave port in Britain, followed by Bristol and Liverpool.
Mid-1700s:	Black citizens could be found among the servant classes but there were a number of notable and accomplished figures from this period including the writer Ignatius Sancho and the abolitionist Olaudah

	Equiano, who published his life story in 1789. This was widely used in the anti-slavery campaign.
1764:	The black population of London is estimated at 20,000 out of a total population of about 700,000.
1771–72:	Somerset case: Lord Mansfield decided that a slave could not be removed from England against his or her will. This signalled the end of slavery in Britain.
1793–1815:	Many black men fought in the Napoleonic wars, including the Battle of Waterloo. Some became Chelsea Pensioners.
1807:	Abolition of the slave trade in Britain.
1834:	Slavery was replaced by apprenticeship in British colonies.
1838:	Full freedom was granted in British colonies.
1901–10:	Black Edwardian music hall players included Belle Davis, Will Garland and the double acts Smith and Johnson and Scott and Whaley.
1912:	The London-based journal *African Times and Orient Review* was launched by businessman and activist Dusé Mohamed Ali with the help of John Eldred Taylor.
1913:	London's first black mayor, John Archer, was elected Mayor of Battersea.
1914:	Britain entered the First World War on 4 August. The newspaper *African Telegraph* was launched by John Eldred Taylor.
1915:	The British West Indies Regiment (BWIR) was formed.
1917:	Sir Harry Johnston publishes *The Black Man's Part in the War*. Walter Tull receives a commission in a British Army infantry regiment.
1918:	The African Progress Union was founded in London; John Archer was its first president. Walter Tull was killed in action in France. The First World War ended.
1919:	Anti-black race riots took place in many British seaports including London, Cardiff and Liverpool. Bermudian seaman Charles Wotten was murdered in Liverpool on 5 June.

BLACK POPPIES Q & A

For *Black Poppies* the following questions were asked by the author to four of his associates: Patrick Vernon OBE, Lorna Blackman, Garry Stewart and Nicholas Bailey.

1. Why do you think the stories of African Caribbean soldiers in the First World Warhave been ignored or forgotten?
2. How/when did you find out that African Caribbeans served in the First World War?
3. Do you think the British school curriculum should include the stories of African Caribbeans in the First World War?
4. Why do you think the British school curriculum mainly focuses on African Americans from history, such as Dr Martin Luther King and Rosa Parks? (Mary Seacole is the only exception).
5. What do you think we should do in 2014–2018 to ensure that young people in Britain are made aware of the important contribution made by African Caribbeans to the First World War?

Here are their responses.

Patrick Vernon OBE
Patrick is the founder of Every Generation Media and 100 Great Black Britons:

The general public have a limited appreciation of the real story and impact of The First World War but when you add the African Caribbean dimensions this is further hidden and whitewashed. This is further reinforced with The Second World War and modern conflicts with the only exception being Johnson Beharry who got a Victoria Cross for his heroic deeds in Iraq.

I was aware of the contribution made by African Caribbeans who served in The First World War probably over fifteen years ago as part of my personal research and exploration around black history. When I made my film *A Charmed Life* about the late Eddie Martin Noble who served in the RAF during The Second World War, I did a lot of background research on The First World War and The Second World War. Finally my father in passing mentioned that one of his relatives served in The First World War.

Most definitely the British school curriculum should include the stories of African Caribbeans in The First World War! It has taken over thirty years campaigning from activists and educationalists to include elements of black history in the curriculum. We still do not have recognition of various West Indies and African regiments and the achievements of heroes like Walter Tull who still has not received his Military Cross.

My campaign 100 Great Black Britons in 2004 – where Mary Seacole was voted as Greatest Black Briton – helped to elevate her in the national curriculum in 2007. However, since then, there has been a gradual attack on race equality in all aspects of the national curriculum leading to a campaign in 2013 where celebrities and over 36,000 people signed a petition to keep Mary Seacole and other aspects of black history in the curriculum.

Politicians, media and mainstream institutions are fixated with the history of struggle and achievement of African Americans which is reinforced with the global brand of USA in all aspects ranging from sports, politics, entertainment and cultural industries. This by default devalues or undermines the black British experience of civil rights and struggle thus influencing policy makers and politicians.

During the The First World War centenary mainstream institutions and funders should work and support community historians and activities. These should be given the platform and resources to share the learning and the history of African Caribbeans in The First World War. Also the government needs to honour Walter Tull with his Military Cross. Finally, we need a media campaign with examples and case studies of African Caribbean contribution to The First World War.

Lorna Blackman

Lorna is the chair of the ACLC Cultural Committee based in Hornsey and Haringey in East London. The aim of the committee is to make all communities aware of the African Caribbean contributions and achievements which have been ignored. Once a race knows their history and achievements they will become motivational, powerful, inspirational, and unbeatable. Lorna, who is also the managing director of the Big People's Theatre Company, has written and directed *Charles: The Last Black Soldier of the First World War*. This was premiered in Hackney in April 2013:

Charles: The Last Black Soldier of the First World War first started off as an essay as part of my A-level English Literature module in 2002. After receiving negative comments from my Literature teacher, I became frustrated. I explained to him that the accounts are real as I had interviewed grandmothers and grandfathers who were witnesses to their fathers and mothers enlisting and fighting for the British Empire. I lost the essay after passing the module but later, while I was clearing up my back room, I found the essay. That same week of finding the essay I read and heard of two more stabbings and shootings of young black men. I really do believe that this play is coming from a spiritual place and I hope that the play will inspire and raise the self-esteem of those that feel that they have no legacy. It begins with a group of soldiers fighting in the trenches, then fast forwards to 2013 in an inner-city school where a young girl is being bullied. She finds a picture of a group of young black soldiers going off to war. Flashback is used to recall the events of these soldiers and also touches on contemporary issues faced by the black community in Britain.

When *Charles: The Last Black Soldier* was performed, during the Q&A audiences believed that the play should be performed in schools to inform and educate. Personally I believe that the British establishment are ashamed about the treatment of black soldiers in both World Wars. They also believe that the subject is too sensitive. I strongly believe that every book that Stephen Bourne has written should be transformed into plays and films and that my play *Charles: The Last Black Soldier* should be on at the West End. I really do believe that drama can open channels for learning and engage even the most challenging students. My teaching is unconventional but successful. This is evident by the pass marks in the LAMDA examinations by my students.

Garry Stewart

Garry is an ex-serviceman. He served with the British Army in the Royal Signals in the Falklands, the Gulf and Germany. In Birmingham in 2008 he launched a black community history group called Recognize. In 2013 he issued a 'call to arms' to others in Birmingham's African Caribbean community to mark the centenary of the First World War. His campaign is called We Were There Too and it was launched at the Library of Birmingham:

> The stories of African Caribbean soldiers in The First World War have not been ignored or forgotten, they have been deliberately whitewashed from the history books due to the political power it would have given people in the Caribbean countries. I have known about their contribution for about two years. So much of this history has been ignored. It's quite shocking. Absolutely the British school curriculum should include the stories of African Caribbeans in The First World War. It is British history and we have to get away from separating black history as if it was something else. I think the British school curriculum mainly focuses on African Americans to make black Britons think, 'OK, we have never had it that bad.' Recognize is a cultural awareness provider and will be co-ordinating a nationwide programme about the black contribution to The First World War. We are currently working on several programmes that will address this issue. We have an exhibition planned to tour schools throughout the UK and there are many other projects planned to raise the awareness.

Nicholas Bailey

Nicholas is an actor who, in 2008, presented the television documentary *Walter Tull: Forgotten Hero* for BBC4:

> They say that 'history is written by the victors' – this begs the question: 'where are the black victorious of World War 1?' We know they exist and their stories lie just beneath the surface of our understanding of the war and its wider resonance. Personally, I think that our understanding of political events is enhanced by our understanding of society and culture. The story of World War 1, as we know it, is simply incomplete without the inclusion of the stories of the African and African – Caribbean participants in that war; at home and abroad. How the black population were affected by and affected the outcome of the First World War is a story whose telling is long overdue.

If 'perception is reality' then historians and leaders of any era control our perception of reality from beyond the grave. There is a responsibility in documenting the present for posterity.

Stories derive their power through creating content and context. The obvious thing to say is that the black soldiers were simply not supposed to be there. When we worked on *Walter Tull: Forgotten Hero*, we discovered that the military establishment believed that enlisting black soldiers in the British Army would result in them turning their guns on their commanding officers, that it was thought that white soldiers wouldn't fight alongside black soldiers and that there was institutional concern about black Allied soldiers taking the lives of white enemy soldiers. Those black service personnel, who gave their youth and their lives for a country that didn't want or expect them to, did so in the full knowledge that the legacy of victory over Germany would probably never be fully shared. To be remembered is to be honoured and empowered.

Their omission from the story of World War 1 was a form of control: by allowing their stories to sublime, history was, in fact re-written. The military establishment re-wrote history in their – and only their – images.

If history is 'us in the past', a picture that doesn't include all relevant, existing information negatively affects our relationship to that past. In the time of Empire, everything was about acquisition, containment, consolidation and the control of hearts and minds. To document was to celebrate; to celebrate was to validate and to validate was to liberate. This doesn't seem to me as if it was ever going to be on the cards for Edwardian black people. In these and other instances, our respect of the history we've been handed hinders rather than helps.

I can remember, clearly, when I first came across the story of the black contribution to the First World War effort. I'd stayed with my brother, in Seven Sisters, in April 1998 and, rising early, I flicked through the local paper that was delivered that morning. In it I stumbled across an article about a commemorative football match, hosted by the late Bernie Grant MP. It was played in honour of Walter Tull, who I'd never heard of before. I was amazed that there was any significant number of black Britons back then, let alone a professional footballer and war hero from Folkestone. I started to try and find out more information and contacted Phil Vasili, who was researching Walter. I thought it would make a great movie! I became passionate about helping tell this amazing story so Phil and I researched Walter for a time and even tried to get a film project off the ground. It's amazing that Walter is now a household name. Hardly anyone had heard of him at the time. There must be other stories like that out there.

The 'Modern British History' curriculum should include these stories, not only for their own sake, but also to deepen our understanding of the important political and cultural elements which frame our understanding of today. I think it's long overdue. We can't call ourselves a multicultural society and purport to be proud of that fact; knowing this information and not sharing it with young people, for their benefit. These stories contextualise and humanise global events and can only resonate with modern learners. The inclusion of these stories would also honour us by connecting us to true British pioneers and positive contributors to the story of the twentieth century.

I must stress that young learners could benefit hugely from learning of the social stories of black non-service personnel. These stories are just as valuable and should be shared. A '*Windrush* myth' exists, placing the start of modern black British history with the passengers of that ship in 1948, even though many of us know that black people have been living, working and dying in Britain for many hundreds of years.

In many ways, our knowledge of Mary Seacole's impressive life and deeds has been assisted by her leading role in the story of Florence Nightingale's life and career. Her impact as a medical pioneer, whose methods were widely adopted, is accepted and celebrated; and rightly so. I believe there are other forgotten lives to be celebrated and hope more black Britons can enjoy similar celebration. I think the British curriculum tends to be based on global, political events involving selected countries. This is certainly what the majority of what I was examined in consisted of. However, there's more to the celebration of these lives than that. I think that those individuals' stories impacted wider society in obvious and immediate ways. Also, their lives were dramatic and their deeds affected those beyond their own community. In addition, they were vocal, challenging the status quo in active ways, during their lifetimes. They couldn't be ignored playing a leading role on the main stage. They called for change, not only in a system but also within the collective culture and psyche.

We mustn't forget the 'quiet storm' of the forgotten black British voices of history. Many of them lacked a platform and were not as vocal on a national stage but their lives are valuable to us and they deserve to be part of the story we hand down to our children and our children's children. The cumulative effect of their lives and deeds is manifested in our desire for equality, integration and tolerance today. The extent to which this legacy has been realised is open to debate but there is a desire within our community to see it realised, extended and sustained.

Make a copy of *Black Poppies* available to every user that can appreciate it; then ask them to go home, read it, share its stories and ask their grandparents if there is anything missing! This book is part of a conversation that we have to have and keep going. The information we've lost through mortality will never be known but I'm convinced that more stories lie hidden in lofts and in the recollections of those who carry vocal accounts in their memories. We need a public archive, debates, social media, lectures, plays, films, anything that helps young people want to take this history forward and own it for themselves. The conversation needs to be spread beyond academic journals and the occasional late-night documentary. The African Caribbean story of the First World War belongs in the mainstream where it can discuss it, share it, add to it and take possession of it.

PART I:

THE ARMED SERVICES

1

LIONEL TURPIN: A LAD IN A SOLDIER'S COAT

When Britain joined the First World War on 4 August 1914, no one could have been more loyal to his king and country than the Guyanese merchant seaman Lionel Turpin. His son, Jackie, recalled in *Battling Jack: You Gotta Fight Back* (2005):

> He felt British. He was descended from slaves taken from West Africa but English was his first language. His schoolbooks were written by British people; he lived under British law; he was brought up to admire British poets and British musicians and British scientists and British politicians and British nobility. His allegiance was to King George V, to his Mother Country and to British people all over the world. When Britain declared war on Germany he felt included.[1]

Lionel Fitzherbert Turpin was born in 1896 in Georgetown, British Guiana, the only colony in South America owned by the British crown. He is described by Caryl Phillips in *Foreigners* (2007) as a young man who 'enjoyed a traditional British schooling in the sugar-rich colony on the north-east coast of South America, but the young lad had a yearning to see the world.'[2] There was a rumour that he left home at the age of 16 because of a falling out with his father. He was still young when he found his way to Britain as a merchant seaman. Jackie said: 'It's likely he worked his passage as a stoker or summat because he couldn't afford to pay his ticket [...] he might have come straight to England then, or he might have tasted the world a little bit as a sailor beforehand.'[3]

According to his army service records, Rifleman Turpin A202638 was just 19 years and 5 months old when he enlisted in August 1915. He gave his address as Collingwood, North Shields. By then he had left the sea and was working as a labourer. For the question 'Are you a British subject?' he replied 'Yes.' Lionel signed up at the York Depot of the York and Lancaster Regiment for the duration of the war. He named his father, John Turpin, as his next of kin. He was then a master carpenter with the city works of 291 Thomas Street, Georgetown, British Guinea (*sic*).

Says Jackie:

Nobody thought the war was gonna last very long, did they? We thought we'd knock out the Germans easy. 'Over by Christmas', was what everybody said. Me dad was sent out in February 1916 with the No. 32 British Expeditionary Force to the Western Front in Europe. He participated in the BEF campaigns of 1916, 1917 and 1918. My dad *was* in the battles of the Somme, then. People have said that from time to time. Trench warfare. Hell on earth. It was a miracle anyone come through that. The Great War lasted for four years and two months and was a bloody free-for-all. They was only lads in soldier coats.[4]

Lionel's army service ended on 3 February 1919 with two medals, two gas-burnt lungs and a shell wound in his back. Says Jackie: 'My dad had survived the worst battles the world had ever seen but a gas shell caught up with him in the last weeks of the war when he was fighting with the 2nd Battalion of the King's Royal Rifle Corps near Arras in northern France.'[5] He returned to Britain for treatment at a hospital in Coventry but, says Caryl Phillips:

They did all they could to help him before discharging the West Indian to a convalescent home near Hill House in the nearby town of Warwick. Although it was clear to the doctors that the mild-mannered coloured soldier was never going to fully recover, Lionel Turpin was eventually allowed to leave the convalescent home and he attempted to find work locally. Lionel stood out in Warwick, for there were no other coloured people in the town, and he was regularly referred to as 'Sam', which was an abbreviation for the more pejorative 'Sambo'. He was equally exotic in nearby Leamington Spa, where the introverted West Indian veteran soon met a local [white] teenager named Beatrice Whitehouse. Beatrice came from a rough, but tight-knit, local working-class family, her father being known as a bare-knuckle prize-fighter.[6]

Lionel and Beatrice were married at Warwick Register Office on 24 December 1921 and he worked as a master moulder at Bissel's Foundry. Jackie recalled:

Most people in those days wouldn't have rented a flat to a black man but an old lady offered me mum and dad a basement flat in Willes Road, Royal Leamington Spa, a couple of miles from Warwick [...] The old lady said my dad was a good patriot. He had come over from one of our colonies to fight for Britain in the war and had got badly wounded doing it, and it was only right that he should have somewhere to live.[7]

The Turpins had five children: Dick, Jackie, Joan, Kathy and Randolph but, as Jackie said: 'My father put up with his war wounds best as he could but his health deteriorated fast.'[8] Says Caryl Phillips:

It was clear that the coloured veteran required full-time care and attention. He was eventually allocated a bed at the Ministry of Pensions Hospital in Birmingham, but on 6 March 1929, nine months after the birth of Randolph, Lionel Fitzherbert finally passed away due to war injuries he had suffered over a decade earlier. His funeral hearse was drawn by four black horses, with six soldiers as an escort.[9]

Lionel was buried in the Brunswick Street Cemetery, Leamington Spa, and his funeral was paid for by the Leamington branch of the British Legion. Says Jackie: 'I think they should put my dad's name, and millions of others like him, on the Roll of Honour with those as lost their lives on the battlefields. All over the world, people died slow unofficial deaths in peacetime beds but it was the war that'd killed them.'[10] Beatrice Turpin, a widow at 25, with five children to raise, was left with a widow's pension of less than thirty shillings a week, and whatever else she could earn cooking and cleaning for people. Jackie tells the story of how a middle-class woman asked if she could adopt him: 'I want to dress him up like a little Indian, in silk pantaloons and a turban, and train him to open the door when people come to the house.' Beatrice restrained herself from hitting the woman but said, 'My son's no slave, and you aren't gonna dress him like a slave. Now sod off!'[11]

Lionel's youngest son Randolph Turpin later became a boxer and is now celebrated as Britain's first twentieth-century middleweight champion of the world. For further information see Scott A.G.M. Crawford, 'Randolph Turpin (1928-1966)', *Oxford Dictionary of National Biography* (Oxford University Press).

Notes

1. Jackie Turpin and W. Terry Fox, *Battling Jack: You Gotta Fight Back* (Mainstream Publishing, 2005), p. 22.
2. Caryl Phillips, *Foreigners* (Harvill Secker, 2007), p. 89.
3. *Battling Jack*, pp. 23–24.
4. Ibid., pp. 25–26.
5. Ibid., p. 26.
6. *Foreigners*, pp. 89–90.
7. *Battling Jack*, p. 29.
8. Ibid., p. 29.
9. *Foreigners*, pp. 90–91.
10. *Battling Jack*, p. 30.
11. Ibid., p. 31.

2

WALTER TULL

Walter Tull is the most celebrated black British soldier of the First World War. Books and documentaries about his life have secured him a place in British history. However, the British Army was reluctant to recruit black soldiers. In the BBC documentary *Walter Tull: Forgotten Hero* (2008), his biographer, Phil Vasili, explained to the presenter, Nicholas Bailey:

> They didn't want men of colour to join. Full stop. The usual ploy used by recruitment people was, if a black guy walked in, tell him to read the eye test from the far end of the room, use a bureaucratic procedure to fail him. But they couldn't do it with Walter. When he turned up he was a known man. This was a guy who had played football for Spurs, Northampton, his face appeared on cigarette cards, in newspapers. It was difficult to fail him on the medical because he's a fit footballer.[1]

Walter was born in Folkestone, Kent, in 1888 to a Barbadian father called Daniel Tull, who worked as a carpenter and joiner, and a white British mother, Alice Elizabeth Palmer. They married in 1880.[2] Daniel's mother, Anna, had been born a slave in Barbados. Daniel had settled in Britain in 1876. Orphaned at the age of 9, Walter and his brother Edward, then aged 11, were placed in the National Children's Home orphanage in Bethnal Green, London. Edward was adopted by a Scottish family and went to live with them in Glasgow. He later qualified as a dentist. Walter served an apprenticeship as a printer, but it was as a footballer that he made his name. Transferring to Northampton Town in 1911, he played 111 matches for them. After the outbreak of the First World War, Walter volunteered for the army and was enlisted in one of the divisions of the Middlesex Regiment that was made up of footballers.

When Walter was recruited into the army in December 1914 he became the 55th member of the newly formed 17th (1st Football) Battalion of the Middlesex Regiment, popularly known as the 'Football Battalion'. This was the result of the Football Association and the War Office joining forces to tap into the game's popularity and using it to attract new recruits. Andrew Riddoch, author of *When the Whistle Blows: The Story of the Footballers' Battalion in the Great War* (2008), explains: 'Professional footballers would join [the army] and encourage club supporters to join up. Some of these men would have been real heroes of the game. So there was an attraction of serving alongside men who they turned up every week to watch.'[3]

Walter was rapidly promoted to corporal and then lance-sergeant. He completed his basic training in November 1915 and the 1st Football Battalion boarded a ship at Folkestone and crossed the English Channel to war-torn France. At first, Walter faced weeks of inactivity and boredom. In a letter to his brother Edward, written in 1916, he described the weeks of waiting before being moved to the front as 'a monotonous life', saying 'most of the boys prefer the excitement of the trenches'. However, in later letters, he talked about the 'carnage' he witnessed on the front line in a war he had come to hate. It was a war in which Walter encountered men in search of glory being slaughtered in their thousands as the Kaiser's army made advances. On a single day in 1916 around 19,000 men who went into battle with him were killed.

As an NCO (non-commissioned officer) Walter went to the front line where he encountered a life of camaraderie and courage amongst much confusion and chaos. Says Chris McNab in *The Pitkin Guide to Tommy: First World War Soldier* (2012):

On the Western Front alone, winding its muddy track down through Belgium and France, this conflict would draw in 4 million British and British Empire soldiers, the vast majority of whom were volunteers in the 'New Armies' or straightforward conscripts, given frequently questionable training and then sent to war in mainland Europe. A total of 1.7 million of them would either lose their lives or suffer debilitating wounds.[4]

In freezing and muddy trenches, Walter fought alongside his comrades in the Football Battalion, but this almost destroyed him. Half of the Football Battalion were killed in action. In April 1916, after six months in France, he was diagnosed with 'acute mania' (shell shock), removed from the front line, and hospitalised. Says Phil Vasili:

> Tull had encountered many situations, legs unsteady, that entailed dig-
> ging deep, drawing upon hidden reserves of strength: the death of his
> mother at 7, the death of his father at 9, the loss of Edward aged 11,
> the brutal hostility of the crowd at Bristol a few months after his League
> debut at Spurs as a 21-year-old. Succumbing to 'acute mania' was, per-
> haps, not the result of his inability to face the unprecedented horror of
> the front-line trenches but an accumulation of the emotional trauma he
> had witnessed and attempted to deal with during the previous nineteen
> years. And on this list of debits we have not included the tension brought
> about by the common, day-to-day racism, a fixture of life in the UK from
> which there was no escape.[5]

In September 1916 Walter returned to action with the 23rd (2nd Football) Battalion of the Middlesex Regiment, which suffered heavy losses in the Battle of the Somme (which had begun on 1 July). In November that year he was recommended for officer training. After the Battle of the Somme the British Army was in need of men of officer material, and Walter fitted the bill. Says Phil Vasili: 'He then returned to Britain for officer training at Gailes in Ayrshire and on 10 May 1917 he was appointed to a commission in the special reserve of officers, before re-joining the 23rd Battalion of the Middlesex Regiment as a Second Lieutenant.'[6] In 1917 it was virtually impossible for a man of African descent to be commissioned an officer. In 1914 *The Manual of Military Law* stated that 'any negro or person of colour' who was not of 'pure European descent' could not become an army officer. Perhaps we will never know for certain which black soldier became the first to be granted a commission as an officer in the British Army during the First World War and yet, in addition to Walter, research has shown that there were other exceptions. These include the Jamaican-born George Edward Kingsley Bemand, though on his 1914 army application form he stated he was of 'pure European descent'. He became a second lieu-tenant in the Royal Field Artillery in May 1915 and was sent to the front in August 1916. He was killed by a shell on Boxing Day 1916.[7]

Historian Jeffrey Green has drawn attention to others, including another Jamaican, Lieutenant Reginald Collins. He took a ship to England and in London joined the 19th Battalion of the Royal Fusiliers. In France in 1916 his officers held him in high regard, and approved his application to be admitted to an Officer Cadet Unit, to train to be an officer in the wartime British Army. The forms were completed in May 1916, and on 18 May he left France to train in Oxford. Collins heard that a third Jamaican contingent was being organised for the British West Indies Regiment (BWIR) (see Chapter 5), and requested to become an officer of it. This was recommended. His file WO 339/62717 (now at the National Archives in Kew) has a comment: 'not suitable to be an officer owing to his colour'. It is dated 11 September 1916. The following year he was appointed second lieutenant with the 6th battalion of the BWIR. He served with them, probably in Egypt and Palestine, and certainly in Italy. Jeffrey Green also acknowledges the neurologist professor J.S. Risien Russell. Originally from British Guiana, and of mixed race, he was a captain in the Royal Army Medical Corps from 1908 to 1918 and worked at the 3rd London General Hospital which was utilised for soldiers requiring special treatment during the First World War.[8]

Walter Tull had special qualities that made him stand out from the crowd and he had demonstrated on many occasions that he could serve with distinction. He had been decorated with the 1914–15 Star, thus making it impossible not to promote him. He is acknowledged as the first black infantry officer in the history of the British Army. As Phil Vasili notes: 'Black soldiers of any rank were not desirable. Military chiefs of staff, with government approval, argued that white soldiers would not accept orders issued by men of colour and on no account should black soldiers serve on the front line.'[9] But Walter's superiors defied government orders.

On the Italian front Walter showed extraordinary courage and leadership when he was ordered to lead a group of men across the fast-flowing river at Piave and attack the forward positions of German and Austrian troops. He led from the front and brought his men back without a single casualty. Consequently Walter was mentioned in dispatches by Major General Lawford, who was commanding the 41st Division, for his 'gallantry and coolness' at the Battle of Piave in Italy in January 1918. Lawford visited the battalion two days later to congratulate them officially and his citation for Walter survives in his family's archive:

I wish to place on record my appreciation of your gallantry and coolness. You were one of the first to cross the river prior to the raid on 1 & 2 Jan. 1918 & during the raid you took the covering party of the main body across and brought them back without a casualty in spite of heavy fire.[10]

Phil Vasili says that Lawford's citation 'acquiesced in formally defying Army regulations which barred men of colour from "exercising any actual command or power".'[11]

On 25 March 1918, during the Second Battle of the Somme, Walter Tull was killed while crossing no-man's-land near the hamlet of Favreuil, which is near Bapaume, France. He was 29. His men tried to recover his body, running into no-man's-land three times, but they were forced back by enemy fire, and his body was never recovered. Nicholas Bailey has described his character: 'From what I gathered, looking into his life, he was a quiet and unassuming man, fiercely intelligent, but physically imposing. He defied all the rules of his time. He never complained, he just let his deeds do the talking.'[12]

Walter's name can be found on the massive Arras Memorial to the missing in northern France, just a few miles away from Favreuil near to where he was killed. Walter's name is one of 34,782 casualties from Britain, South Africa and New Zealand with no known grave which are on the Arras Memorial.

When his brother Edward received the telegram informing him of his younger brother's death, he described it as the worst moment of his life. In a letter written to Edward in April 1918, Walter's Commanding Officer, Major Poole, described how he behaved on the battlefield: '[he] was very cool in moments of danger and always volunteered for any enterprise that might be of service [...] His courage was of a high order and was combined with a quiet and unassuming manner.'[13]

In recent years memorials, books and television documentaries have ensured Walter Tull his place in British history but he did not receive the Military Cross, in spite of the recommendation made by his commanding officer of the 23rd Battalion. Interviewed by Melissa van der Klugt in the *Independent* (2 February 2013), Phil Vasili said:

The award, should it happen, will rebalance the scales of justice. I examined similar awards to subalterns in the same theatre of war and I'm convinced there is no rational reason for rejecting Tull's recommendation other than to have awarded the Military Cross would have admitted to the powers that be that they had broken their own rules in commissioning him. His promotion signified the absurdity of the thinking that white soldiers would not respect black officers.

It would take another twenty-three years for another black soldier to become an officer in the British Army when, in 1940, London-born Charles Arundel Moody joined the Queen's Own Royal West Kent Regiment.[14]

Notes

1. Phil Vasili, interviewed by Nicholas Bailey, *Walter Tull: Forgotten Hero*, BBC Scotland for BBC4, 13 November 2008.
2. For further information see Phil Vasili, 'Walter Tull (1888–1918), footballer and army officer', in *Oxford Dictionary of National Biography* (Oxford University Press, September 2004) and *Walter Tull, 1888–1918 Officer, Footballer* (Raw Press, 2010).
3. Andrew Riddoch, interviewed by Nicholas Bailey, *Walter Tull: Forgotten Hero*.
4. Chris McNab, *The Pitkin Guide to Tommy: First World War Soldier* (Pitkin Publishing, 2012), p. 1.
5. Phil Vasili, *Walter Tull, 1888–1918 Officer, Footballer* (Raw Press, 2010), p. 160.
6. Vasili, *Oxford Dictionary of National Biography*.
7. For further information about George Edward Kingsley Bemand see www.greatwarlondon.wordpress.com; the Great War Forum (www.1914-1918.invisionzone.com); and Alison Moise's letter to *Southwark News* (7 March 2013), p. 24.
8. '066: Lieutenant Reginald Collins of Jamaica', www.jeffreygreen.co.uk. See also Jeffrey Green, 'James Samuel Risien Russell (1863–1939), neurologist', *Oxford Dictionary of National Biography* (Oxford University Press, October 2010).
9. Phil Vasili, interviewed by Danielle Weekes, *New Nation*, 3 November 2008, p. 4.
10. Finlayson Family Collection quoted in Vasili, *Walter Tull, 1888–1918 Officer, Footballer*, p. 180.
11. Ibid.
12. Nicholas Bailey, interviewed by Danielle Weekes, *New Nation*, 3 November 2008, p. 4.
13. Dan Lyndon, *Walter Tull: Footballer, Soldier, Hero* (Collins Big Cat, 2011), p. 49.
14. Stephen Bourne, *The Motherland Calls: Britain's Black Servicemen and Women, 1939–1945* (The History Press, 2012).

3

ALL THE KING'S MEN

After Britain joined the First World War, black recruits from different backgrounds could be found in all branches of the armed services. Page 471 of the *Manual of Military Law* (1914), stated that 'any negro or person of colour, although an alien, may voluntarily enlist' and when serving would be 'deemed to be entitled to all the privileges of a natural-born British subject'. A note indicates that this passage relates to enlisted persons 'and prohibits their promotion to commissioned rank'. According to the historian Jeffrey Green:

> This shows that African descent enlisted people should not be promoted to be officers. It is not crystal clear, which explains why Walter Tull etc were commissioned. I know of no evidence that black men were not enlisted; when conscription came in 1916, all British born males were surely in the pool. My understanding is that the distinction was drawn between officers and rankers, the former having authority over the latter. The conscription laws applied to *all* male citizens and the *1914 Manual of Military Law* said the volunteers could enlist. The manual did not bar anyone. I suspect recruiting officers may have had different opinions but there seems to have been no law that excluded black men from being enlisted. We are being told a story backwards, without knowing how many blacks were subject to conscription 1916–1918, an assumption is made that, because officers could not be black, rankers could not be black. There are enough photographs of blacks in standard regiments to show that they were

not siphoned off into 'ethnic' regiments such as the British West Indies Regiment. Imagine a recruiting station somewhere in Britain before conscription. A bunch of lads turn up and volunteer, and are processed. How many sergeants or officers would say that one (or more) of the group of pals could not be accepted? After conscription was legislated, anyone presenting the papers would be processed. Excluding blacks would upset the other reluctant recruits who were only there because they had to be there. Turn down one and the others would be aggrieved.[1]

From 1914 black Britons volunteered at recruitment centres and were joined by West Indian and other colonials. They travelled to the Mother Country from the Caribbean and other parts of the British Empire at their own expense to take part in the fight against the Germans. Their support was needed, and they gave it. Soon after the war started, soldiers from Nigeria, The Gambia, Rhodesia (now Zimbabwe), South Africa, Sierra Leone, Uganda, Nyasaland (now Malawi), Kenya and the Gold Coast (now Ghana) were recruited. Many saw active service in their home continent, taking part in the campaigns to capture the German-controlled territories of Togo, Cameroon, German South West Africa (now Namibia) and German East Africa (now Tanzania). Of a population of some 30,000,000 in the African colonies of the British Empire, 55,000 men served as combatant soldiers, and many hundreds of thousands more as carriers and auxiliary troops. An estimated 10,000 were killed or died while serving. A total of 166 decorations were awarded to Africans. Many of them helped to defend the borders of their countries which adjoined German territories and later played an important role in the campaigns to remove the Germans from Africa. Throughout the war 60,000 black South African and 120,000 other Africans served in uniformed Labour Units.[2]

It is a little known fact that the first shot fired in the First World War did not take place in Europe or the Pacific, but was fired by an African, Alhaji Grunshi, of the Gold Coast Regiment, on 12 August 1914. Africa was the site of the first military action by British land forces and Grunshi fired the shot in the German colony of Togoland, which was isolated from the rest of the German Empire. It had the British Gold Coast to the west, French Dahomey to the east, and French West Africa to the north. The area being strategically vital to the defence of Germany's overseas empire, troops of the Gold Coast Regiment entered Togoland from the British Gold Coast and advanced on the capital, Lome. An advance patrol of the regiment encountered the German-led police force in August 1914 near Lome and the police force opened fire. Alhaji Grunshi returned fire and became the first soldier in the British service to fire a shot in the First World War. In 1940 *The Times* reported details of what happened:

It was on the Gold Coast that the first shot was fired by a British soldier in the last War. It came from a rifle carried by a dusky warrior whose name was Sergeant Alhaji Grunshi, and whose face bore the tribal scars of a people familiar only to the traveller who has penetrated into the hot savannah land north of the Colony of Ashanti [...] Sergeant Grunshi was a member of the Gold Coast Regiment, West African Frontier Force, and was one of the contingent of troops which marched into the then German dependency of Togoland shortly after the war was declared. There was little show of resistance to this invasion, but at Lome, some miles from the capital, a few Germans, ensconced in a factory, opened fire on a British patrol. This fire was promptly returned by Sergeant Grunshi and the first bullet to leave his rifle (although neither Alhaji nor any of his companions realized it at the time) signalized the opening of four years of bitter hostilities in the course of which the Empire was to lose more than 1,000,000 dead. During that war hundreds of Gold Coast men followed Sergeant Grunshi on active service in West and East Africa.[3]

The first white soldier of the British Army to fire a shot was Corporal Edward Thomas of the 4th Royal Irish Dragoon Guards. This took place on the Western Front in France on 22 August 1914. Grunshi survived the war, having fought in three African campaigns and he was mentioned in dispatches on 5 March 1918. On 13 March 1919, as a sergeant, he was awarded the Military Medal for his part in the East African Campaign. The first confirmed Commonwealth casualty under fire was Grunshi's comrade, Private Bai, who was killed in action on 15 August 1914, probably at Agbeluvoe, 50 miles north of Lome. Unlike Grunshi, nothing is known of Private Bai (only one name is given). Private Bai's name is engraved on the memorial at Kumasi in Ghana.

In Britain in 1914 the response to the campaign to join up was overwhelming and at recruiting offices up and down the country small numbers of black and mixed-race men were successful at joining the army partly because the recruitment centres were not made aware that they were supposed to be discouraging black recruits. The historian David Killingray says that 'whether or not a man was accepted into the ranks appears to have depended largely upon the attitude of individual recruiting officers and also the degree of colour of the recruit'.[4] In December 1914 Gilbert Grindle, a principal clerk at the Colonial Office, wrote: 'I hear privately that some recruiting officers will pass coloureds. Others, however, will not, and we must discourage coloured volunteers.'[5]

Information about the lives of black servicemen in the First World War is difficult to find. There are hardly any interviews, and identifying soldiers and sailors from army and navy records is a hit-and-miss task because ethnicity was only rarely recorded. Their stories are fragmented, and this has made the recording of their wartime experiences an almost impossible task. This is not the case with the Second World War because large numbers of black servicemen and women who survived the 1939–45 conflict lived long enough to be interviewed about their experiences. In the case of others, like Cy Grant and E. Martin Noble, they wrote and published their memoirs.[6]

Various sources mention names and offer brief details of black army recruits. In *Under the Imperial Carpet* (1986) David Killingray listed several black recruits who were accepted by the British Army. These include John Williams who joined in 1914, fought in France, was wounded four times and decorated with the Distinguished Conduct Medal (DCM), the Military Medal, the French Military Medal, the Cross of St George and the French Legion of Honour; Henry Solomon, a former pupil of St Paul's School (London) who enlisted in 1918; and George Williams, twice wounded and gassed in France, according to the *Sierra Leone Weekly News* (18 January 1919). Killingray also mentions 'the fascinating self-styled "African Savage", LoBagola, who claimed to be a black Jew from West Africa, [who] joined the British Army in 1918 via the recruiting office in New York.'[7] LoBagola later wrote an autobiography, the sensationally titled *An African Savage's Own Story* (1930), in which he published his British Army Certificate of Discharge. This confirmed that Private LoBagola indeed served with the Royal Fusiliers, but many of the stories he related in the book are questionable. Though he did serve in the British Army, Lobagola was not an African but an American, according to David Killingray and Willie Henderson's detailed study of his adventurous life in *Africans on Stage* (1999). LoBagola was Joseph Howard Lee of Baltimore, born 1888, died 1947. The authors say that 'By adopting an African identity, LoBagola was able to exploit his blackness in a way that opened doors that would otherwise have been closed to an African American.'[8]

Exhibitions about Britain's black community can bring to light information that has not previously been brought to the public's attention. In 2008, in its exhibition 'From War to Windrush', the Imperial War Museum acknowledged the army service of a mixed-race working-class Londoner, No. 207431 Private Harold Brown. He was born in Poplar in East London in 1899. His parents were John Benjamin Brown, a West Indian seaman, and Elizabeth Cross, a white Londoner; they were married in 1898. In the 1901 census 2-year-old Harold is living with his mother and baby sister Ada in London's dockland. Ten years later, in the 1911 census, schoolboy Harold and his family are still living in docklands, at 4 Watford Road, Tidal Basin, Victoria Docks. Brown served as a private with the Royal West Surrey Regiment and his bravery was recognised with two certificates of gallantry and in 1918 the award of the Military Medal. After he was demobilised in 1919, Harold worked as a seaman and then as a docker at the Royal Albert Docks in London's East End until he died in 1955. The Imperial War Museum have in their documents collection two photographs of Harold, including one of him in uniform, as well as his two Divisional Certificates of Gallantry.[9] 'From War to Windrush' also included the Trinidadian Cyril Blake (1897–1951). When Cyril enlisted in the Merchant Navy in the First World War he was one of thousands of men from the Caribbean who entered the service to fill the places of British men who had left the Merchant Navy to join the Royal Navy.

Another source of information about black soldiers in the First World War is the Caribbean Roll of Honour website (www.caribbeanrollof-honor-ww1-ww2.yolasite.com). For example, it includes brief sketches about recruits such as (Richard) Henry Bascombe, a young Trinidadian who made his own way to England to enlist. He was a private in the 3rd King's Liverpool Regiment and was wounded. He was subsequently recommended for the DCM, but there is no record of this being awarded. Bascombe was killed in London on 5 August 1916 as a result of a collision with a motor lorry while cycling. He may not have died on a battlefield, but he is commemorated on the Port of Spain's Cenotaph and buried in the Pembroke Dock Military Cemetery in Wales.

The *Oxford Dictionary of National Biography* includes Charles Kay's biography of the ship-owner Sir Herbert Gladstone McDavid (1898–1966). Herbert was born in Liverpool, and though he looked white (a photograph of him can be seen in the National Portrait Gallery's online collection), his maternal grandfather was born of African descent in Antigua, West Indies. Herbert enlisted in the Liverpool Scottish Battalion at the beginning of 1917, but he was captured and made a prisoner of war (he was reported missing on 31 July 1917 and officially accepted as a POW in Germany on 25 September 1917). Says Kay: 'Quickly mastering German, he acted as an interpreter, failed in an escape attempt, and by late 1918 was virtually running the prisoner-of-war camp. For his outstanding services he was awarded the Meritorious Service Medal.'[10] Herbert was a prisoner of war for seventeen months until he was repatriated in 1919.

Richard Smith's informative contribution to the *Moving Here* website includes information about several black soldiers. They include Charlie Cooper, a boxer, who joined the Manchester Regiment in 1917, and Egbert Watson, a Jamaican, who settled in London's Camden Town and then enlisted as a gunner in the Royal Garrison Artillery. Watson served in France for two years until he was invalided out at the end of 1917. Another Jamaican, Alonzo Nathan, was a seaman who lived in Cardiff and enlisted in the Army Service Corps before being transferred to the British West Indies Regiment. Smith also provides references to documents in the National Archives which relate to some of the soldiers.[11]

The Memorial Gates website includes the story of Winston Churchill Millington who distinguished himself during his service with the British West Indies Regiment. Winston was born in Barbados in 1893 and in 1897 he moved to Trinidad with his father, who was a teacher. Winston was one of the first to volunteer for the BWIR's 'B' Company in Trinidad. In December 1916 they sailed from England to Alexandria in Egypt, on their way to fight in the Palestine Campaign. This campaign was far away from the main conflicts of the First World War in Europe. However, the battle here against the Turks was a vicious affair because, according to Winston, 'the Turks were ferocious fighters'. It was not long before the machine-gun crews of the BWIR were tested. They were sent into action against a large body of Turkish soldiers and showed great coolness and self-discipline under fire. The commanding officer of 162 Machine-gun Company praised the work of the West Indian gunners: 'The men (in the machine-gun section) worked exceedingly well [...] showing keen interest in their work, cheerfulness, coolness under fire and the ability to carry it out under difficulties.' General Allenby also highlighted the machine-gun crews' outstanding achievements. He wrote to the Governors of Jamaica and the other British West Indian colonies: 'I have great pleasure in informing you of the excellent conduct of the machine-gun section of the BWIR during two successful raids on the Turkish trenches. All ranks behaved with great gallantry under heavy rifle fire, and contributed in no small measure to the success of the operation.' In these battles a number of soldiers distinguished themselves through their bravery. One of them was Winston Millington. When the Turks attacked, the rest of his gun crew were killed by enemy fire, but Winston continued to fire his gun for several minutes. He was awarded the DCM for his gallantry and coolness in action.[12]

Another website, liverpoolremembrance.weebly.com, includes the story of Ernest Quarless who was one of many 'boy soldiers' who lied about their ages and joined up during the First World War. The website states that the youngest soldier proven to have served on the Western Front was Edward Barnett, a 13-year-old lad from Salford. He enlisted in the 7th Manchester regiment in May 1915 but a week later his age was discovered and he was discharged. The very next day he managed to sign himself up with the 19th Manchester's. He lasted four months at the Western Front before his real age was discovered again, and he was sent home. Ernest Quarless was born in Liverpool in 1905 to John Isiah Quarless, a Merchant seaman from Barbados, and Elizabeth, the daughter of a Jamaican sailor. John served in the Merchant Navy throughout the war. Somehow Ernest managed to join the British West Indies Regiment in July 1917 when he was just 11 years and 9 months of age: 'The website is not trying to prove that Ernest Quarless broke any records as the youngest serving soldier, we have no idea if he saw action, our only intention is to highlight his remarkable story.'[13]

The Unknown Soldiers

The Imperial War Museum in London has a number of photographs in their collection that show black soldiers in the First World War, most of them are members of the British West Indies Regiment, but – with only a handful of exceptions – none of them are named. So we have some visual record of black servicemen, but their identities and experiences have not been recorded. The historian Jeffrey Green has found black individuals in photographs and books who have not been identified, and will remain 'unknown'. These include the soldier in Peter Hart's *1918, a Very British Victory* (2008). On page 356 Hart quotes from the Imperial War Museum's interview with Second Lieutenant

William Tobey, of the 16th battalion of the Lancashire Fusiliers [96th Brigade, 32nd Division] recalling early August 1918. A corporal had been injured and he called for three volunteers to go forward towards the Germans and collect the corporal under covering fire. 'I said to the men, "I want three volunteers to go and carry Corporal Cave back here!" Three men stepped forward, one of which was the only black man in the battalion.' The identity of this man is also unknown.[14]

Frank Dove

Black Britons who joined the army came from different social classes. Frank Dove was the mixed-race son of Francis 'Frans' Dove, a middle-class barrister from Sierra Leone in West Africa, and his English wife Augusta Winchester. They were married in London in 1896. Frank was born Francis Sydney Dove in London in 1897 and in November 1916, at the age of 19, he was studying law at Oxford when he was called up for service in the British Army. According to his army service record his physical development was 'excellent' and he confirmed that he was a British subject. The only clue to his African heritage is the naming of his father, Frans Dove, as next of kin, and Accra, West Africa is given as his father's address. Frank gave his home address as Brighton. On entering the army, Private Frank Dove joined the elite Royal Tank Corps and received the Military Medal for his bravery at the Battle of Cambrai in 1917. This was the first breach of the German lines in over three years. His army service record shows that Frank was 'wounded on duty' in the field in December 1917 and granted leave. In June 1918, at the age of 20, he proceeded to Britain for a Commission in the Cadet Unit of the Royal Air Force (RAF). His entry card into the RAF, dated 18 July 1918, confirmed that he smoked (inhaled) and suffered from seasickness. He was demobbed in 1920 and died in 1957.

Albert James

Albert James came from Liverpool's working class. He was the mixed-race son of Edward James, a Bermudian seaman who had settled in the Toxteth area of Liverpool in the 1850s and married his English wife, Harriet Gates, in 1873. They had six children. Two of their sons served in the First World War: William (born 1883) in the Merchant Navy and Albert (born 1888) in the Royal Field Artillery. Says Albert's grandson, the historian Ray Costello: 'Albert enlisted at the beginning of the First World War, leaving a 1-year-old son and a wife, Ethel, who was five months pregnant, such was the pull of patriotism.'[15] Ray adds that one of Albert's sisters also supported the war effort: 'Auntie Flo was a seamstress during the war making caps and uniforms in the Lybro Factory in the Kensington area of Liverpool. Lybro was owned by Quakers and was one of the few firms that would employ black women.'[16] Albert died in Liverpool in 1962.

Joseph Highsmith Jr

Joseph Highsmith Jr was the son of the black British-born music hall artiste Josephine Morcashani and her African American husband. Joseph was born in London in 1894 and worked with his mother on the stage. At the outbreak of the First World War he was stranded with his mother in Berlin, but fortunately the American authorities agreed to treat them both as American citizens on the basis of Joseph Sr's American nationality. With new passports they were able to leave Berlin and travel to Britain. Joseph Jr joined the King's Royal Rifles on 11 December 1915. On his entrance forms he gave his profession as 'cinema operator' and his address as 2 Newington Crescent, Newington Butts, SE1. He was wounded in France on 31 July 1916, and discharged as unfit for further service in November. However, he re-enlisted in July 1917 and served a further thirty-four days. Joseph Jr survived the war, and died in the Radcliffe Infirmary in Oxford in 1959.

West Indians of African descent and Africans also served in ordinary British regiments, and they included the following:

Charles Williams

Charles Augustus Williams was born in Barbados in 1879 and was a member of a large family who adopted the surname of the sugar plantation owner who employed them. Lying about his age, young Charles enrolled with a merchant steamer as a cabin boy at Bridgetown dock and spent the next twenty years travelling the world. He later described his years in the Merchant Navy as a happy time. In 1914 Charles settled in Britain. Stephen D. Smith described Charles in his biography of his son, the comedian Charlie Williams, as

> A handsome man, over six feet tall [...] He was extremely strong, fearless and a most suitable candidate for the forces [...] Entranced by the promises of glory, Charles enlisted in the Royal Engineers and within a matter of days found himself in the realities and horror of the trenches of the Somme. He was no stranger to hardship and difficult living conditions and so he found it relatively easy to comply with the rigours and discipline of life in the forces, but the memories of the futility of war and the obscenity of death in conflict were to live with him for ever.[17]

Charles served his king and country with pride. He enlisted in November 1915 and was discharged one year later. He was decorated for his bravery (he received the Victory and British medals), but throughout his life his modesty forbade him to talk about his experiences of the First World War. Says Smith:

> The 'secret' was only uncovered from a chance meeting with one of his former compatriots. He was a very brave man who achieved great popularity amongst his fellow soldiers [...] He was lucky. He managed to survive the war without suffering the ignominy of wounds, but like so many others he was left with a legacy of frostbite and a condition with the unpleasant sounding name of 'trench feet' which was to haunt him for the rest of his life.[18]

After the war, Charles made his home in Royston, a small mining village near Barnsley in South Yorkshire. He worked in the pits and died in 1944.

Louis Achoy

Louis Achoy's service was brief. Born in Port of Spain, Trinidad, the 19-year-old sailor was recruited in Newcastle-upon-Tyne by the Northumberland Fusiliers, 1st Tyneside Irish, on 6 November 1914. But just over a month later, on 22 December, he was discharged under Kings Regulations, Para 392 (iii) and the following reason was given:

'Not likely to become an efficient soldier. Coloured man.' A medical officer noted that Louis suffered from 'cardiac weakness' and also described him as a 'coloured man'. It is difficult to know if it was Louis's race or his heart condition that led to him being discharged so quickly, and yet his loyalty to king and country is without question. Also recorded, under 'distinctive marks', are descriptions of his tattoos. In addition to his left arm bearing the 'head and bust of lady', it also included a British flag. His right arm bore the King George V's crown. Louis did not survive the war. Though he returned to the sea as a merchant seaman, and served on the ship *Messina*, he died at the age of 22 on 23 September 1918 in the Seaman's Hospital in Greenwich. The cause of his death was heart failure.

Joe Clough

Joe Clough was born in Jamaica in 1885 and orphaned at an early age. As a child he was employed by Dr White, a Scottish doctor, to look after his ponies. When Joe was 18, Dr White offered him the opportunity to travel to Britain as his servant and companion. Young Joe accepted; he never saw Jamaica again. In Edwardian London Joe would drive Dr White around in his coach and horses, but the doctor was keen to acquire a motor car, which were becoming popular. Consequently Joe learned to drive and became the doctor's chauffeur. In 1910 Joe successfully applied for work as a driver with the London General Omnibus Company. He passed his bus driving test and began driving a bus on the No. 11 route between Liverpool Street and Wormwood Scrubs. Joe remained in contact with Dr White and said that when he visited his former employer the doctor always treated him with respect and entertained him in the drawing room. In 1911 Joe married a white British woman, Margaret Baker, the daughter of a publican. They had two daughters, Margaret (1912) and Jeanie (1915). In the 1911 census, Joe is described as a 'Motor Bus Driver' and living with his wife in Portland Road in the Notting Hill area of London.

In 1915 a patriotic Joe enlisted in the Army Service Corps based at Kempston Barracks in Bedfordshire. A letter dated 4 June 1915 from his employers, J. & S. Hinsby, Carriers and Motor Bus Proprietors, of St. Neots in Huntingdonshire, endorsed his application: 'Mr Joseph Clough has been with us for three and a half years as Motor Omnibus Driver. We have found him a most careful driver, not having had an accident from any fault of his during the whole time. We have also found him strictly honest.'

In a War Office minute dated January 1917 Sir Arthur Sloggett, the Director-General of Army Medical Services, stated the following: 'Neither woman nor coloured troops could be used in Field Ambulances or convoys to replace the medical personnel. Strength, coolness and courage, in addition to technical training, are required.'[19] However, Joe proved Sloggett wrong by driving a field ambulance for four years in Ypres on the Western Front, the location of some of the war's bloodiest battles.

When John Brown interviewed Joe for *The Un-Melting Pot* (1970), he said he was proud that everywhere he went on the front line he was liked and respected: 'No trouble, no trouble at all nowhere. Nobody mentioned my colour. I was like a king there. They even made me captain of the cricket team.'[20] However, Joe did recall an incident at a corporals' dance in Kempston Barracks just after the First World War when a captain demanded drunkenly, 'Who gave that damned nigger an invitation? Get him out of here.' Joe withdrew but later he received a regimental apology. He was also granted the freedom of Kempston Barracks for the rest of his life.

Demobbed in 1919, Joe settled in Bedford with his family. He worked as a bus driver until after the Second World War. On Remembrance Day each year between the wars, Joe would drive the 'poppy' bus, a bus that collected money for the Earl Haig Poppy Fund. He refused wages as a mark of respect for the soldiers he had served with. From 1949 he had his own taxi cab business until he retired in 1968. He died in 1976 at the age of 91.

In 1970 John Brown described Joe as a private person who

> Has total acceptance in Bedford. No doubt the fact that he was unique helped make it so [...] Skill and integrity in his profession: a constant and kindly involvement in community life, giving readily, demanding nothing: and with these things, a pattern of family life to disarm the harshest critic. What he and his wife have made between them is not a small thing. They live deservedly in peace and in the town's esteem.[21]

Selvin Campbell

Selvin Campbell, who was also known as Alexander Sylvan Campbell, was born in Jamaica in 1897 and served with the British Expeditionary Force

(BEF) in the First World War. He claimed he had left Jamaica at the age of 15 or 16 and travelled with a doctor to Holland. He arrived in Britain at the outbreak of the war, and joined the army. He later described himself as 'a very good singer and a dancer' who entertained the troops in France with both ragtime and straight songs. Mustard gas affected his lungs and, after the war, Alexander tried to find work as a professional singer, but he was 'unlucky'. However, he has been described as a 'street singer' and his daughter, the London-born Clementina, born in 1927, inherited his musicality and became the internationally acclaimed jazz singer Cleo Laine. She later told an interviewer: 'I knew very little about him. Except that he left Jamaica after a violent row with his father. But he was such a storyteller that one couldn't believe everything he said.'[22] Cleo confirmed that he served with the BEF during the First World War, and that he was a:

Real Victorian papa, who laid down strict standards of behaviour which I and my brother and sister had to follow. We didn't mind – we loved him. He was a wonderful singer and a dandy who never lost this Don Juan side of his personality, and he flirted well into his eighties. Everybody knew him as 'the darkie with the pipe,' and the word didn't bother him at all. To him it was like being called 'mate'.[23]

In her autobiography, *Cleo* (1994), Cleo Laine remembered her father:

Standing up proud as punch when he came to hear me sing, digging people in the ribs, as he told them, 'That's my daughter up there!' Although he never told me himself, I know that he always had a twinkle in his eye when he saw me perform.[24]

Selvin Campbell died in 1980.

Frederick Njilima

Frederick Njilima was born in Malawi (then colonial Nyasaland) in the 1890s. He spent the years between 1909 and 1919 in the United States and Europe. Frederick's father, Duncan Njilima, took part in the John Chilembwe Uprising in Nyasaland of January 1915. Like other African businessmen of the time, Njilima felt that the labour laws of white colonials discriminated against him. After his capture, Duncan

Njilima was hanged by the British colonial authorities for his part in the uprising in which Europeans had been killed. When their father was executed, Frederick's brother Matthew wanted nothing more to do with Nyasaland under colonial rule. However, Frederick was keen to pursue his education at St John's College, Cambridge University, and to further his father's business interests. Bishop Wilfred Hornby, who had once lived in Nyasaland and employed Duncan as a house servant in the 1890s, advised Frederick that he should atone for his father's participation in the uprising before he could recommend him to St John's. He told him that the best way to do this was to join the British Army and fight in the war. Frederick Gresham, as he chose to be called in the army, enlisted on 23 January 1917 at the age of 22. He gave his address as 9 Dartmouth Street, Westminster. In his army service record he describes his profession as 'scholar'. Private Gresham trained in the Irish Rifles in Winchester and Nottingham, and was then posted to the Machine Gun Corps at Ypres where he served bravely in France in 1917 and 1918. Wounded near Reims on 27 May 1918, he was sent to the Cambridge Hospital, Aldershot and was awarded the Military Medal and received a letter of commendation from the British Crown. In October 1919 he returned to Nyasaland with a 20 per cent disability pension.

The Navy

During the First World War, many merchant seamen joined the Royal Navy, thus enabling many black men to replace them in the Merchant Navy. Consequently the Merchant Navy began recruiting seamen from the West Indies to support the war effort, but others could be found in Britain's seaports, such as Cardiff and Liverpool. Black merchant seamen from Britain, the West Indies and Africa were among the thousands who died in the service of king and country when German U-boats attacked their ships, bringing supplies to Britain. *The Times* of 13 June 1919 acknowledged that 'there are over a thousand coloured men out of work in Cardiff, most of them sailors, and it has to be remembered to their credit that during the war they faced the perils of the submarine campaign with all the gallantry of the British seamen.'[25]

One of those men was Marcus Bailey, who was born in Bridgetown, Barbados in 1883. From the age of 19 in 1903 he served on thirty-four merchant and fishing vessels, mostly as a cook, until he received his seaman's certificate in 1912. Four years later Marcus joined the crew of the Royal Naval vessel HMS *Chester* as an able seaman. The ship had been launched on 8 December 1915 and entered service in May 1916, only three weeks before the Battle of Jutland. HMS *Chester* was part of the 3rd Battle Cruiser Squadron. Marcus was serving on the ship when it was hit by seventeen 150mm shells during the Battle of Jutland. Twenty-nine men were killed and forty-nine wounded. Marcus continued to serve in the Merchant Navy after the war.

In 1913 in Fleetwood, Lancaster, Marcus married Lily McGowan, a white British woman of Irish descent, and they had three children: Francis (aka Frank) (1914), James (1915) and Lilian (1918). Most of the time Marcus was away from home at sea when the children were small, so their memories of him were sketchy. However, Lilian did later recall a small but vivid incident from the early 1920s that brought home to her, and her brothers, the realisation that they were mixed race:

> She and her two older brothers bought a Christmas card to send to their father at sea. When they brought the card home, their Auntie Maud (who was looking after them in the absence of their parents) took one look at it and insisted: 'We can't send that to him.' Jim was ordered back to the shop to change it. Lilian could not understand her aunt's fussiness. But Aunt Maud was quite right, for on the front of the children's original card was a golliwog.[26]

Sadly, when they were still very young, the three children were orphaned. Their father died on 27 January 1927, aged 43, and their mother died soon after. Lilian was just 9 years old when she was separated from her two elder brothers and sent to a convent. However, all three of the mixed-race children served their country in the armed forces during the Second World War. Lilian joined the Women's Auxiliary Air Force (WAAF) while her brothers followed in their father's footsteps and served in the navy, but tragedy was to strike the family again. James became an able seaman in the Merchant Navy and was serving on the SS *Western Chief* when he was killed in action at the age of 24 on 14 March 1941. He is remembered with honour on the Tower Hill Memorial in London. Said Lilian:

My brother Jim had been reported missing, but I hoped against hope that he had been picked up as I knew he sailed in a convoy. The survivors of the 'Western Chief' were picked up, but Jim was not amongst them. A few letters; they were only young boys after all, a couple of photos, and one visit from them in 1936, were all that I had left of family life.[27]

Among the many black merchant seamen who gave their lives for Britain in the First World War was John Liverpool, a 27-year-old Kruman from Freetown in Sierra Leone. He was killed on 5 May 1917 after a torpedo attack on his ship, the SS *Harmattan* (London) but, says Ray Costello in *Black Salt: Seafarers of African Descent on British Ships* (2012):

> When his family attempted to claim compensation, the problem of nation-ality raised its head. Enquiries were made by the Freetown Commissioner of Police, who concluded he was not a British subject and therefore could not be considered. He thought Liverpool was a Liberian subject brought to Sierra Leone when very young by his parents. His sister, Nimneh Kon, stated that she was born in Liberia, but that her brother John was born in Freetown, Sierra Leone [...] It seemed that Liberian-born Kru residing in Freetown (Liberia being another part of the Kru national territories, since European colonial boundaries often ignored local tribal borders) were not officially classed as British subjects, in spite of members of that tribal group coming and going at will, crossing borders that may have had little relevance to them.[28]

John Liverpool's family may not have succeeded in claiming compen-sation, but this seafarer who was killed in action in the service of the British Empire has not been forgotten. His name can be found, along with his 'true' African surname, Torbotoh, on the Tower Hill Memorial in London. He is 'Remembered with Honour' and on the Commonwealth War Graves Commission's website he is described as having been born in Sierra Leone, the son of the late Gbengoh.

Notes

1. Stephen Bourne, interview with Jeffrey Green, London, 23 November 2013.
2. 'First World War Participants: Africa', www.memorial-gates-london.org.uk
3. 'The Gold Coast Mobilized', *The Times*, 25 March 1940, issue 48572, p. 7.
4. David Killingray, 'All the King's Men? Blacks in the British Army in the First

World War, 1914–1918', Rainer Lotz and Ian Pegg, editors, *Under the Imperial Carpet: Essays in Black History 1780-1950* (Rabbit Press, 1986), p. 170.

5. PRO CO 318/333/50043, 'West Indian Contingent'. Min. by Gilbert Grindle, 21 December 1914.

6. Stephen Bourne, *The Motherland Calls: Britain's Black Servicemen and Women 1939–1945* (The History Press, 2012).

7. Killingray, 'All the King's Men?', p. 177.

8. David Killingray and Willie Henderson, 'Bata Kindai Amgoza ibn LoBogola and the Making of *An African Savage's Own Story*', Bernth Lindfors, editor, *Africans on Stage: Studies in Ethnological Show Business* (Indiana University Press, 1999), pp. 228–65.

9. Harold Brown (1899–1955), Imperial War Museum Documents 5579: Private Papers.

10. Charles Kay, 'Sir Herbert Gladstone McDavid (1898–1966), shipowner', *Oxford Dictionary of National Biography* (Oxford University Press, September 2010). See also Ray Costello, *Liverpool Black Pioneers* (The Bluecoat Press, 2007).

11. Richard Smith, 'Caribbean Migration to Britain during World War One,' *Moving Here: Migration Histories*, www.movinghere.org.uk.

12. 'First World War Participants: Caribbean', www.memorial-gates-london.org.uk

13. 'Liverpool and Merseyside Remembered – Ernest Arthur Quarless', www. liverpoolremembrance.weebly.com

14. Jeffrey Green, by email, 23 November 2013.

15. Ray Costello, by email, 29 November 2013.

16. Ibid.

17. Stephen D. Smith, *Charlie: The Charlie Williams Story* (Neville-Douglas Publishing, 1998), pp. 15–17.

18. Ibid.

19. Richard Smith, *Jamaican Volunteers in the First World War* (Manchester University Press, 2004), p. 79.

20. John Brown, *The Un-Melting Pot: An English Town and its Immigrants* (Macmillan, 1970), p. 24.

21. Ibid., pp. 24–25.

22. Cleo Laine interviewed by Michael Church in *Caribbean Beat*, Issue 13, March/April 1995.

23. Ibid.

24. Cleo Laine, *Cleo* (Simon and Schuster, 1994), p. 279.

25. 'Race Rioting at Cardiff', *The Times*, 13 June 1919, issue 42125, p. 9.

26. Ben Bousquet and Colin Douglas, *West Indian Women at War: British Racism in World War II* (Lawrence Wishart, 1991), p. 128.

27. Ray Costello, *Black Liverpool: The Early History of Britain's Oldest Black Community 1730–1918* (Liverpool: Picton Press, 2001), pp. 53-54.

28. Ray Costello, *Black Salt: Seafarers of African Descent on British Ships* (Liverpool University Press, 2012), p. 144.

4

NORMAN MANLEY

Before he died in 1969, Norman Manley, who served as Jamaica's Chief Minister from 1955–59 and as Prime Minister 1959–62, began writing an autobiography. He did not complete it, but when the *Jamaica Journal* published some extracts in 1973, these included Norman's detailed account of his experiences of the First World War. This record now serves as a rare example of a black soldier's first-hand account of life on the front line.

Norman Washington Manley was born in Roxburgh in the parish of Manchester, Jamaica in 1893. Both his parents were mixed race of African, Caribbean and Irish descent: Thomas Manley, a planter and produce dealer, and Margaret Ann Shearer, whom Norman described as 'near-white'. By 1909 Norman's parents had died, and eventually he moved to England where his sister Vera had studied music and become a music teacher. In 1914 Norman became a Rhodes Scholar and entered Jesus College, Oxford, to read law.[1] In September 1915, with his younger brother Douglas Roy Manley, known as Roy, he enlisted as a private in the Deptford Royal Field Artillery.[2]

In his autobiography, Norman describes the 'strange circumstances' he faced when he joined the Royal Field Artillery in Deptford, a working-class area of South London, situated across the River Thames from the East End. Seventy per cent of the recruits he encountered were cockneys 'with a view of life all their own':

I got to know them very well and a great affection developed between us. They were first-class thieves and would rob your last farthing if you gave them the chance, but for kindness and generosity I have never met their equal. If you were broke and did not have a cigarette to smoke they would not hesitate to give you one if they had two. They came to look on 'Bill', as they called me, as a great oracle and I was to settle a thousand arguments about everything under the sun. When deadlock occurred, the watch-word was 'Let's ask Bill!' I was careful to plead ignorance unless I really knew and could explain, and so preserved respect and confidence. They shewed innate courtesy, I suppose because we liked each other, and soon found out that I did not like being called 'Darkie' as came natural to them, and I have heard a real tough guy get hold of a new arrival, a casualty replacement, who automatically called me 'Darkie', and take him aside and say, 'Don't call him that – he doesn't like it. We call him Bill and we like him!'[3]

Norman also recalled the time he fell ill, and how his cockney comrades took care of him, nursed him and looked out for him. If he felt too unwell for guard duty, someone took his place.

When Norman served with his comrades on the Western Front in France, he remembered it as an 'odd life', once you had grown used to its hardships:

Hard work, dull work, poor food and hard living quarters, to say nothing of the eternal misery of body lice which were found everywhere that soldiers lived [...] in spite of all these things, there was a strange and fascinating irresponsibility about the life of a private [...] Nothing in the future gave you concern. Your job was to do your job as a soldier and stay alive if you could. You blessed each day, you prayed to be spared some fear-raising experience like being caught in a severe German artillery barrage or a gas attack with gas shells, but that aside, to be alive was to have a future and worry about the future had no place.[4]

When Norman joined the Royal Field Artillery he was attached to of the most mobile part of it: the ammunition supply. Within a month of enlisting he was a lance corporal, or bombardier as they were called in the artillery, and by the time he left France in January 1916 (after four months of training), Norman had been promoted to corporal. In stark contrast to the comradeship and friendship he had experienced with the working-class cockneys when he was a new recruit, he came up against violent prejudice from the rank and file who:

> Disliked taking orders from a coloured NCO [non-commissioned officer] and their attitude was mild by comparison with that of my fellow NCOs. Corporals and Sergeants resented my sharing status with them. They were more spiteful and later conspired to get me into trouble. It was only the Officer class that I could expect to behave with ordinary decency and both aspects of this phenomenon I fully understood.[5]

Norman was disgusted with the racist attitudes he confronted on the Western Front, including that of a sergeant who placed him on a charge. The sergeant's rage, recalled Norman, 'born of prejudice', knew no limits. Norman explained to an officer that the NCOs resented his status because of his colour and 'there would never be a peaceful relationship'. Consequently Norman gave up his stripes, joined another regiment, and reverted to the rank of gunner (gun-layer):

> I remained as a gun-layer till I left the Army in 1919. I was the fastest gun-layer in the battery. A gun-layer, by the way, is the man who oper-ated a fairly complex unit that sets the gun dead on target when it is fired [...] In my new unit I started with a clean sheet, did not repeat my earlier mistakes and built up a most agreeable relationship with everybody. They respected and liked me and would follow my leadership in any circum-stances. I liked them as men and as human beings.[6]

In 1916 Norman was sent to the Somme, which he described as 'one of the bloody battles fought for four months with a limited advance of about 6 miles at a cost of half a million casualties.'[7] At Ypres he was involved in battles with his brother Roy who was wounded in early 1917. After returning to his division, and his brother Norman, Roy was killed in a German bombardment at the Ypres front on 26 July 1917. He was 21 years old. Norman later recalled:

> I was not there when they struck [...] It was just at dusk when they opened a terrific artillery fire on the wood. In five minutes half our men were dead or wounded. Those who could ran out and among those running was my brother Roy, carrying on his back a man thought to be wounded – it turned out he was dead – and then he too fell, killed by a shell that burst a

little distance off and sent a small fragment of its casting straight into his heart. We buried him with others next day, all wrapped in blankets and placed in a field already established in anticipation of the battle, not far from where we had our camp. I cannot speak of how I felt. We were good friends and I was to be lonely for the rest of the war – lonely and bitter.[8]

Roy's war grave can be found in Poperinghe New Military Cemetery in Belgium. The death of Roy devastated Norman, who described him as a young man who intended to make writing his career and had:

A fine mind and a large and generous love of life and people [...] I have never in my long life met anyone who found it so natural and habitual to get in touch with perfect strangers, people seen on the street – men and women – and to get lost in a talk in which they revealed all they could of themselves [...] For him every walk in a city by himself was a potential short story taken from life.[9]

In other parts of the war section of his autobiography, Norman vividly evoked life on the front line, such as the time thousands of guns opened fire at a precisely timed second of time:

It has to be imagined to realize how the world can dissolve into one vast sound, so that nothing exists except the continuous unbroken rhythm of sound, like a great wave drowning every feeling and every emotion – sound broken every minute by the vast roar of our 18 inch guns, and punctuated constantly by the staccato tattoo of a couple dozen seventy eight pound-ers sounding a practised roll like super machine-gun fire – but mostly just sound – that you could feel that it enveloped you and bore you up.[10]

He also described how he avoided death. On one occasion he heard the roar of a coming shell:

They come with an awesome sound as their velocity was just a little less than sound. I knew from the increasing horror of the noise that I was in for a near shave and at the last split second dived for the ground and felt the shake of the air as it passed so near to me [...] Then I felt myself show-ered with earth and the noise of an exploding shell and came to realise that I was actually at the bottom of the crater made by the shell [...] My escape was miraculous.[11]

In 1917 Norman took part in the Battle of Passchendaele, also known as the Third Battle of Ypres or 'Passchendaele'. The battle took place on the Western Front between July and November. He recalled the horror of seeing

> A lot of dead people, three-parts buried by mud – you spotted them by an emerging hand or foot, or even a head. It was indescribable [...] As a battle it was the great failure of the War. It is estimated it cost the British 750,000 men killed and wounded. The cream of the British Army and of the men who volunteered in 1914 to 1916 when conscription was introduced.[12]

Norman was on leave in London on Armistice Day, 11 November 1918:

> I was in Hyde Park that night with an estimated crowd of one million. It was over, but I could get no sense of joy. Long anticipation of some events leaves you cold and practical when they arrive [...] I remembered my fallen friends but the number was so great that each loss was reduced by some strange rule of feeling. I thought of the future of mankind but it did not seem that the spirit that had fused in unity with the slogans about 'The war to end war' and 'Make the world safe for Democracy' was going to survive the passions and hazards of peace.[13]

Norman was awarded the Military Medal for his war service. After 1919, when Norman was demobilised, he returned to Jamaica and served as a barrister. He married his cousin, Edna Manley, in 1921. In the *Oxford Dictionary of National Biography*, T.E. Sealy summarises him as a big man:

> Whether in things of the intellect, in the skills of the law, in the arts of life, or in public dedication, his commitment was total and unselfish. The foundations of parliament and the law in Jamaica owe much of their strength to his legal and constitutional skill, and as in the troubles of 1938 when he first assumed a public role he continued at all times to resist the dangers of national turbulence and divisiveness.[14]

Notes

1. T.E. Sealy, 'Norman Washington Manley (1893–1969), lawyer and chief minister of Jamaica', *Oxford Dictionary of National Biography* (Oxford University Press, 2004).

2. Roy had been a pupil at Felstead, an English public school, and his British Army Service Record confirms that he was living at 48 Cathcart Road, Earl's Court, in London. He gave his next of kin as his older sister Vera Holme Manley of Heamoor in Cornwall. Vera had been in England in 1911 when the census identifies her as a 20-year-old student of music boarding at Felden Street in Fulham. She married Dr Ludlow Murcott Moody, a younger brother of the community leader Dr Harold Moody, in 1924. See also Douglas Roy Manley, British Army The First World War Service Records, 1914-1920, www.ancestry. co.uk

3. Norman Manley, 'The Autobiography of Norman Washington Manley', *Jamaica Journal*, vol. 7, no. 1–2 (March–June 1973), p. 6.

4. Ibid.

5. Ibid., p. 7.

6. Ibid.

7. Ibid.

8. Ibid., p. 8.

9. Ibid.

10. Ibid.

11. Ibid.

12. Ibid., p. 9. A statistic for the Battle of Passchendaele: Tyne Copt war cemetery contains memorials with the names of nearly 34,000 British soldiers who died after 15 August 1917.

13. Ibid., p. 14.

14. T.E. Sealy, *Oxford Dictionary of National Biography*.

5

BRITISH WEST INDIES REGIMENT

This chapter is based on the script of the television documentary *Mutiny*, written and researched by Tony T. and Rebecca Goldstone at Sweet Patootee – producers of educational media resources. In the 1990s Tony and Rebecca embarked on their research of the then little-known and rarely acknowledged British West Indies Regiment. After a long search (before email and internet) they tracked down and interviewed the last surviving veterans of the regiment.

I first watched *Mutiny* when it was shown on Channel 4 in 1999, and I am indebted to Tony and Rebecca for bringing this story of the Caribbean experience in the First World War to my attention and allowing me to borrow extensively from their script.

The First World War is usually viewed as a predominantly white European conflict but, in fact, over one third of the men who found themselves under imperial British command were non-whites. They were mostly drawn from Asia, Africa and the Caribbean, but also Britain. These are now forgotten men who willingly served their king and empire. Some of them even died for the cause. In 1914, in spite of a relationship with Britain that included slavery, followed by colonial rule, the people of British Guiana (later known as Guyana) and the West Indies remained loyal to the empire and the island they described as their 'Mother Country'. Cerene Palmer was born in Jamaica and remembered what her grandmother told her about the 'Mother Country'. Her grandmother, Tammar Palmer, had been born in the Victorian era and died at the age of 89 in the 1970s. Cerene said:

> My grandmother used to say: 'I'm going to England', and we say 'but you don't know anybody there!' [laughs]. She said she don't mind because she is British and England is the Mother Country. The term Mother Country was while slavery was abolished and we became a single British colony, in the British West Indies, and we'd say 'England is our Mother Country'. It could have come from Queen Victoria because my grandmother used to refer to her a lot. She was so proud of 'Mrs Queen Victoria'. She used to curtsey every time she referred to 'Mrs Queen Victoria'.[1]

In Jamaica the young Marcus Garvey, who became an influential political leader, encouraged support for Britain. On the eve of the war, in Jamaica, he founded the Universal Negro Improvement Association. He hoped that, by serving king and country, and making an honourable sacrifice on the battlefields, the soldiers would earn Jamaicans and other West Indians equality and political power after the war. In 1914 there was high unemployment in the Caribbean and West Indians were working for starvation wages. In *Mutiny* (1999), 106-year-old Eugent Clarke explained why he volunteered at the age of 21: 'It wasn't easy to find work in Jamaica, and the pay was nothing. It was mainly cultivation. Only one or two factories were in the island. The people couldn't get work.'[2]

Immediately after the war broke out, men from the colonies, including British Guiana and the Caribbean islands, demonstrated their willingness to support their 'Mother Country' and enlist in the army. Some black men even stowed away on ships bound for England. However, the War Office was not enthusiastic about recruiting black volunteers and threatened to repatriate any black men who arrived in this country with a view to joining up. There were concerns that, if a black soldier was given a gun, he could be a source of danger to his white comrades, and not the enemy. It was felt that their colour would make them conspicuous on the battlefields. Some believed that German propaganda would ridicule the British Army for recruiting black soldiers because the whites were not good enough to fight. In spite of this, West Indian volunteers continued to come forward and were recruited, though some who tried to enlist were turned away.

In Trinidad the young C.L.R. James, who became an influential historian and political philosopher, decided he wanted to support the British in their hour of need. In his memoir, *Beyond a Boundary* (1963), James described how his desire to 'see the world' took him to a recruiting office. In 1918 he was just 17 and still a schoolboy at Queen's Royal College in Port of Spain, for which he had received a scholarship:

We had been deluged with propaganda [...] There were two ways by which one could go: the public contingent [...] and the Merchants' Contingent [...] rumour was [...] the merchants selected only white or brown people. But though I was dark, I was widely known as a coming cricketer [...] I was tall and very fit [...] I went down to the office where one of the big merchants, perhaps the biggest of all, examined the would-be-warriors. Young man after young man went in, and I was not obviously inferior to any of them in anything. The merchant talked to each, asked for references and arranged for further examination as the case might be. When my turn came I walked to his desk. He took one look at me, saw my dark skin and, shaking his head vigorously, motioned me violently away [...] White boys from the school joined the public contingent as commissioned officers and came back to the college to see us with chests out and smart uniforms and shining buttons. When the masters heard what had happened to me some of them were angry, one or two ashamed, all were on my side. It didn't hurt for long because for so many years these crude intrusions from the world which surrounded us had been excluded. I had not even been wounded, for no scar was left.[3]

In 2001 C.L.R. James's biographer Farrukh Dhondy said that there was no evidence that James felt he had missed out by not taking part in the First World War:

In fact, he spoke of it only as the beginning of a new barbarism in Europe, taking millions of young lives in a destructive orgy unparalleled in history. In speeches he time and again used the statistics of death in combat and of the Holocaust to demonstrate how the civilized world in the twentieth century went repeatedly down the path of barbarism, into the cesspool of racial and nationalistic murder. The irony was that James who had been reading the work of Wilfred Owen and Siegfried Sassoon, made no connection between the public school ethic which he embraced and the slaughter of the trenches.[4]

By 1915 the War Office and the Colonial Office realised that they could not ignore the requests of West Indian men to join up. However, when the Colonial Office proposed a separate West Indian contingent to aid the war effort, the War Office refused. Eventually the Colonial Office, with the intervention and support of King George V in April 1915, were able to raise a West Indian contingent. Lord Kitchener, the Secretary of State for War, did not want black recruits and his rationale for this was that they would be more visible on the battlefield. There were also concerns that black soldiers would outshine their white comrades on the battlefields, and this would give them the confidence to demand self-determination in the colonies of the British Empire in the post-war world. However, Kitchener was forced to accept King George V's request, but he insisted that he would decide where they would be employed. The king wanted to show the world a united empire in wartime. He was also concerned that the exclusion of black troops might undermine British rule in the colonies. In spite of the objections of the War Office, approval was given on 19 May 1915 and small units of black soldiers were brought together at the North Camp in Seaford, Sussex. Consequently the British West Indies Regiment (BWIR) was formed as a separate black unit within the British Army but no black soldier was to rise above the rank of sergeant.[5] All the commanding officers of the BWIR had to be white. One of the white officers was Lieutenant Colonel Charles Wood-Hill who championed and defended the BWIR all through the war and in 1919 described their formation in his unpublished war memoir:

It is almost unnecessary to state that the West Indian Colonies are admittedly some of the most loyal and devoted members of the Empire. On the outbreak of war, there was a great desire throughout the West Indies to participate in the struggle, and various offers of Contingents were refused by the War Office; but nothing daunted, individual West Indians paid their passage from the West Indies and joined up in British Regiments, and their numbers were considerable. In addition, various gifts of money for the Red Cross, aeroplanes, etc., poured in from all sources. As the war progressed, it became apparent that it would be a long one and the man-power question became acute. Eventually, the War Office accepted the Contingents of men from the West Indies and the British West Indies Regiment was brought into being by Royal Charter.[6]

On 26 October 1915 the British West Indies Regiment was established and later formalised by Army Order Number 4 of 1916. This was passed on 3 November 1915 and the Order stated that the regiment would be recognised as a corps for the purposes of the Army Act. By the war's end in November 1918, the BWIR had registered 15,204 men and had rejected 13,940. Of the total accepted 10,280 (66 per cent) came from Jamaica. Says Jeffrey Green:

> The majority were Jamaicans but recruits came from most if not all the islands, as well as British Guiana (Guyana) and British Honduras (Belize), and from Caribbean communities in Panama, Canada and the USA [...] Of the first 4,000 men enlisted 1,033 were labourers, 657 were cultivators, 356 carpenters, 245 bakers, and there were 42 police constables and 40 teachers.[7]

In Jamaica, Eugent Clarke volunteered for the BWIR:

> They were recruiting and when I went there to join up I saw some big stout fat men coming back. They said they had failed the test. So I felt like turning back because I was just a liccle weakling. I said, 'Look how the big fat men they return. I should also turn back'. But, just like a voice said to me, 'Go on and see'. When my aunt saw me coming she was frightened because she saw me in a uniform and I didn't leave home in a uniform. She said to me – she had a friend in the yard named Rosie – she said, 'Rosie, look, Eugent's gone and become a soldier. You're only a German bait.' That is what she said to me. I said, 'Never mind, I have to go for England. I like the old England.'[8]

In March 1916 Eugent left his home in Jamaica and began a journey to England on the ship *Verdala*. It carried 1,115 black soldiers and twenty-five white officers. They were the 3rd Jamaica contingent of the BWIR. The soldiers wore lightweight tropical uniforms on a ship that was unheated. Worse was to come. To avoid German submarines, the Admiralty ordered Eugent's ship to take a detour to Halifax, the capital of Nova Scotia in Canada, but it ran into a blizzard. Says Eugent:

> When we arrived in Halifax nearly the whole battalion was frost-bitten. It was the first time we'd ever seen snow. We the soldiers going to England didn't have on those warm clothes like what the army in Europe wear.

We were just wearing thin khaki. After we were caught in the snow they issued the thick khaki clothes, the uniform that the English soldiers wear. By that time we were frost-bitten already.[9]

Lieutenant Colonel Wood-Hill spoke up for his men, and recalled in his war memoir: 'many West Indians lost their lives from pneumonia on board ship from the West Indies to England and this was entirely due to the fact that they were unsuitably clothed – no warm underclothing, no overcoats and sick accommodation totally unsuitable.'[10] Six hundred men were badly frost-bitten and 106 remained in Halifax to have amputations. Eugent Clarke was among the 200 who were sent to Bermuda to convalesce: 'When we got to Bermuda, I was just creeping. I couldn't walk. Just creep on my knees. After we were there six weeks some of us feel strong.'[11] After he recovered, Eugent continued his journey to Europe.

The British press kept quiet about the Halifax disaster, but it was reported in the Canadian newspapers which were accessed and read throughout the West Indies. The authorities realised that they had to act quickly or face severe disruption of the recruitment process in the Caribbean, especially Jamaica where the soldiers had been recruited. Consequently the press was allowed to print the official version of the incident. The Admiralty was criticised for making a terrible and avoidable blunder. The Halifax incident undermined the recruitment campaign in the West Indies, so it had to be temporarily suspended. On 29 June 1916, when some of the victims returned to Jamaica, they were greeted by a curious and sympathetic crowd. Jamaica's *Gleaner* newspaper (3 June 1916) reported on 'The Return of Our Wounded'. After the disaster, large numbers of women and children attended recruiting meetings but relatively few men did. Women in Jamaica were asked to assist the recruiting process by encouraging men to volunteer. At the same time, the recruitment officers adopted a more vigorous strategy of house-to-house visits.[12]

By the time the BWIR had crossed the Atlantic, the British Army was fighting on several fronts and these included Africa, Europe, the Mediterranean and the Middle East. Three battalions of the BWIR were sent to Egypt and in July 1916 the BWIR's 3rd and 4th battalions were sent to the Western Front in France and Belgium to work as ammunition carriers. But it was decided that the fighting on the front line was to be done by the white soldiers. Consequently the soldiers of the BWIR spent much of their time at labouring work, loading food and ammunition, laying telephone wires and digging trenches. This was important work, for the BWIR played their part at battles like the Somme and Ypres by helping to sustain their white comrades, but at no time were they permitted to fight as a battalion. Lieutenant Colonel Wood-Hill tried to persuade his superiors to reverse their decision, but his efforts fell on deaf ears. He later said:

> As soon as the War Office had enough West Indian shell-carrying Battalions in France, the latter Battalions were turned into pure and simple labour Battalions. In 1917, further efforts were made to try and get the War Office to allow some of these men to fight [...] I was informed that it was the considered opinion that the fighting qualities of West Indians were doubtful and that it was therefore preferred to use them on shell carrying and labour duties.[13]

Black soldiers rarely took part in front-line fighting but when George Blackman was interviewed by Simon Rogers in the *Guardian* in 2002, at the age of 105, he revealed that he did fight. Rogers described George as almost certainly the last man alive of the BWIR (Eugent Clarke had passed away earlier in 2002). Born in Barbados in 1897, George was keen to support the war effort, so he lied about his age to join the British West Indies Regiment. Singing calypsos like 'Run, Kaiser William, Run', George said he wanted to join up 'because the island government told us that the King said all Englishmen must go to join the war'.[14] George served as a private in the 4th BWIR. Rogers says there is evidence that some Caribbean soldiers were involved in actual combat in France. George remembered what life was like in the trenches and fighting alongside white soldiers:

> It was cold. And everywhere there were white lice. We had to shave the hair because the lice grow there. All our socks were full of white lice [...] They called us darkies. But when the battle starts, it didn't make a difference. We were all the same. When you're there, you don't care about anything. Every man there is under the rifle. The Tommies said, 'Darkie, let them have it.' I made the order: 'Bayonets, fix,' and then 'B company, fire.' You know what it is to go and fight somebody hand to hand? You need plenty nerves. They come at you with the bayonet. He pushes at me, I push at he. You push that bayonet in there and hit with the butt of the gun – if he is dead he is dead, if he live he live. The Tommies, they brought

up some German prisoners and these prisoners were spitting on their hands and wiping on their faces, to say we were painted black.[15]

The BWIR battalions were also allowed a combat role in the Middle East. Some served in Mesopotamia (today's Iraq). The battalions in Egypt that moved into Palestine served as infantry.

Eugent Clarke served at Ypres:

> The war was raging in Europe. The Germans never ceased fire. Night and day, bombs. We had to live under the earth in dugouts. The Somme was bad, man. You stuck in the mud. We had a rough time in that country. The wind would cut you. How we cold. We had to have double socks. Every soldier had to wear double or the cold would have killed us.[16]

The horror of trench warfare was brought home to the BWIR's Guyanese recruit Gershom Browne who, at the age of 101, recalled the following incident in *Mutiny* (1999):

> I was in the trench when they started to shell. Shells coming, man. What happened with my friend, Eustace Phillips. So, he was on the hilltop and he was just going into the Bivouac [shelter] when he and the shell met together. Dead! And those things always make you feel you shouldn't have been in the army. I didn't get to see his funeral because when you're in the front line you don't have no funerals. They just make a hole and sometimes four or five of you go in the hole, you know.[17]

When the end of the war finally came in 1918, Gershom Browne vividly recalled the relief felt by everyone: 'We saw the [signal] flags flashing, and then we began to read. That is, our signallers began to read the flashes being flashed "Armistice Declared!" It was a joyous night-time, that particular night.'[18] During the First World War, sixteen soldiers from the BWIR were decorated for bravery but by the end of the war the BWIR had lost 185 soldiers (killed or died of wounds). A further 1,071 died of illness and 697 were wounded. In Seaford Cemetery there are more than 300 Commonwealth War Graves and nineteen of the headstones display the crest of the BWIR.

In his unpublished memoir, Lieutenant Colonel Wood-Hill summarised the problems faced by the BWIR and took the opportunity to criticise their treatment at the hands of the War Office:

In writing these notes on the history of the British West Indies Regiment, there are two factors that have had a disastrous effect on the life of the Regiment, from the very day of its birth to the signing of the Armistice. Firstly, the War Office have never taken the Regiment seriously, and had always held the opinion that the West Indian would never be any use as a soldier, and that his fighting qualities are doubtful, and that in a word, he is 'gutless.' Hence the employment of West Indians as shell carriers and finally as labourers. Secondly, the entire absence of any West Indian Government organization behind the Regiment, either in the West Indies, in England, France, Italy, Egypt, Mesopotamia or East Africa. Had the West Indian Islands been federated, the whole history, life and being of the Regiment would have been altered. Out of evil may have come good. This is the first time on record that West Indians from various Islands have had an opportunity of meeting together, and the dismal tragedy of this Regiment has taught them a painful lesson. The West Indies must be federated under one Governor and Government with adequate representation in London, and then a future lies before them.[19]

However, according to Richard Smith in the journal *Caribbean Studies* (2008), Wood-Hill was an ambiguous character, a reactionary whose obsession with military honour and discipline drove his championing of the BWIR. After the war he made it clear in a letter to the West India Committee that he firmly hoped military discipline had made Jamaicans immune to political radicalisation.[20]

At the end of the war some members of the BWIR from all fronts were transferred to a military camp in Cimino in the port town of Taranto, Italy. Taranto was an important communications centre and three battalions of the BWIR (8, 10 and 11) were based there. It has been estimated that around 8,000 West Indian soldiers waited at Taranto for a passage home and they were forced to wait for a very long time. Lieutenant Colonel Charles Wood-Hill later commented, 'never were West Indians so humiliated and badly treated'.[21] With the war's end, it seemed that the comradeship between black and white soldiers had gone. Gershom Browne, one of the West Indian soldiers at Taranto, later recalled: 'Since we came here, we couldn't understand why these British soldiers they didn't seem to want any attachment with us. We had always seemed to get on good together in Egypt.'[22] The alienation felt by the BWIR intensified when they were denied the pay rise given to their white British comrades. Their complaints about this act of discrimination were ignored. Finally, on

6 December 1918, the situation began to escalate. The BWIR justifiably resented being ordered to wash the dirty linen of white British soldiers *and* Italian labourers. When they were ordered to clean the latrines [toilets] of their fellow white soldiers, they flatly refused to obey this command, and this led to an angry confrontation. After 6 December, open rebellion continued for a further three days. In spite of the mutineers surrendering after four days, all the soldiers of the BWIR were forced into disarming. Then the situation worsened when the British Army appointed a South African, Brigadier General Carey Bernard, to take over the camp and restore order. He was a man who refused to treat West Indians as equals. He referred to them as 'niggers' and complained that, as 'niggers', during the war, the British Army had treated them better than they had a right to expect. He refused to allow the West Indian soldiers to go to the cinema and use other recreational facilities. Eugent Clarke remembered him as a 'rough man': 'Oh, Lord! With him you couldn't even go to the gate, much less so to town.'[23] The Brigadier General court-martialled the mutineers and most of them were sentenced to either three or five years in prison. While white soldiers were being demobbed, their West Indian comrades were kept virtual prisoners for almost a year after the Armistice.

By September 1919 the BWIR had returned home, but they were not given a hero's welcome like their British counterparts. White colonials in the Caribbean feared them and refused to welcome them. However, the soldiers of the BWIR were left with a new-found feeling of rebellion against their white oppressors. Soldiers of the BWIR were convinced that the only way forward was to fight for the end of the British Empire, independence for their islands, and for black people to govern themselves after they had returned home to the Caribbean. As Simon Rogers wrote in the *Guardian* (6 November 2002):

> The empire changed [...] The [BWIR] soldiers who emerged were so politicised that island governments encouraged them to emigrate to Cuba, Columbia and Venezuela. Those who returned to their countries altered everything [...] A secret colonial memo from 1919, uncovered by researchers for a Channel 4 programme on the Taranto mutiny, showed that the British government realised that everything had changed, too: 'Nothing we can do will alter the fact that the black man has begun to think and feel himself as good as the white.' In a sense, history was rewritten. That meant no celebrations, no official acknowledgement.[24]

It is understood that most of the service records of the British West Indies Regiment were destroyed in an air raid during the Second World War, but we do know that many of the soldiers of the BWIR were decorated as heroes. The BWIR had five Distinguished Service Orders (DSO), nine Military Crosses (MC), two Member of the British Empire medals (MBE), eight Distinguished Conduct Medals (DCM), thirty-seven Military Medals (MM) and forty-nine mentions in dispatches.

Notes

1. Stephen Bourne, *Mother Country: Britain's Black Community on the Home Front 1939–1945* (The History Press, 2010), p. 122.
2. Eugent Clarke, *Mutiny*, Illuminations in Association with Sweet Patootee, researched and written by Tony T. and Rebecca Goldstone. Channel 4, 10 October 1999.
3. C.L.R. James, *Beyond a Boundary* (Hutchinson, 1963), pp. 40–41.
4. Farrukh Dhondy, *C.L.R. James* (Weidenfeld and Nicholson, 2001), p. 11.
5. The British West Indies Regiment is not to be confused with the West India Regiment – often wrongly referred to as the West Indies Regiment – which was raised in 1792 and disbanded in 1927. For more information see Brian Dyde, *The Empty Sleeve: The Story of the West India Regiments of the British Army* (Hansib, 1997) or the DVD resource researched and written by Tony T. and Rebecca Goldstone: *The First Black Britons*, Sweet Patootee for BBC Education, 2005.
6. Lieutenant Colonel Charles Wood-Hill, 'A Few Notes on the History of the British West Indies Regiment', unpublished, 1919, p. 1.
7. Thanks to Jeffrey Green for access to his unpublished essay 'The British West Indies Regiment' (2012). The statistics quoted here were found by Jeffrey Green in Glenford Howe's PhD thesis, later published as *Race, War and Nationalism: A Social History of West Indians in the First World War* (Ian Randle, 2002).
8. Clarke, *Mutiny*, Illuminations in Association with Sweet Patootee, researched and written by Tony T. and Rebecca Goldstone. Channel 4, 10 October 1999.
9. Ibid.
10. Wood-Hill, p. 2.
11. Clarke, *Mutiny*, Illuminations in Association with Sweet Patootee, researched and written by Tony T. and Rebecca Goldstone. Channel 4, 10 October 1999.
12. Glenford Howe, *Race, War and Nationalism – A Social History of West Indians in the First World War* (Ian Randle, 2002), pp. 80–81.
13. Wood-Hill, p. 5.
14. Simon Rogers, 'There were no parades for us', *Guardian*, 6 November 2002.
15. Ibid.
16. Clarke, *Mutiny*, Illuminations in Association with Sweet Patootee, researched and written by Tony T. and Rebecca Goldstone. Channel 4, 10 October 1999.
17. Gershom Browne, *Mutiny*, Illuminations in Association with Sweet Patootee, researched and written by Tony T. and Rebecca Goldstone. Channel 4, 10 October 1999.
18. Ibid.
19. Wood-Hill, p. 8.

20. Richard Smith, 'West Indians at War', *Caribbean Studies*, vol. 36, no. 1, January–June 2008, pp. 224–31.
21. Lieutenant Colonel Charles Wood-Hill, 'A Few Notes on the History of the British West Indies Regiment', unpublished, 1919, p. 10.
22. Gershom Browne, *Mutiny*, Illuminations in Association with Sweet Patootee, researched and written by Tony T. and Rebecca Goldstone. Channel 4, 10 October 1999.
23. Eugent Clarke, *Mutiny*, Illuminations in Association with Sweet Patootee, researched and written by Tony T. and Rebecca Goldstone. Channel 4, 10 October 1999.
24. Simon Rogers, 'There were no parades for us', *Guardian*, 6 November 2002. The memo referred to by Rogers was written by Gilbert Grindle, Assistant Under-Secretary at the Colonial Office in London and quoted by the makers of *Mutiny* (1999).

6

A JAMAICAN LAD, SHOT AT DAWN

Herbert Morris was born in 1900, the son of William and Ophelia Morris of Riversdale, St Catherine, Jamaica. He was just a lad of 16 when he volunteered for war service. He was recruited in Jamaica for the 6th Battalion of the British West Indies Regiment (6BWIR) and, as he wished, he was sent to the trenches of Flanders where his superiors noted in their records that he 'behaved well'. Less than a year later, Herbert's battalion was stationed close to the front line, building trench parapets under heavy and continuous gunfire and serving a battery of eighty-pound guns at 'Essex Farm' near Poperinge, in the Ypres Salient. Says Richard Smith in *Jamaican Volunteers in the First World War* (2004): 'In the fifteen-day barrage preceding the main Allied thrust on 31 July, 2297 British guns fired over four million shells – four times the number fired prior to the attack on the Somme. The Germans responded in kind and the 6BWIR experienced daily casualties.'' A Catholic priest who lived close by recalled that some members of the 6BWIR became afraid of the guns and often showed signs of disorientation during the shelling. Eventually Herbert's nerves gave way, and the shell-shocked youngster fled from the trenches. He went absent without leave and was reported to have stayed on the run for two days before being arrested. His capture was inevitable because it was almost impossible for deserters to remain at liberty in France, and to find a way back home to England. Richard Smith says that Herbert was picked up at Boulogne and given fourteen days' field punishment:

On 20 August, having seen seven of his comrades become casualties, Herbert absconded again, jumping from the lorry taking him to his battery. He was arrested, once more at Boulogne, when he entered a rest camp with no ticket of leave. Morris had clear symptoms of battle fatigue or 'shell shock'. He pleaded to the court 'I am troubled with my head and cannot stand the sound of the guns. I reported to the Dr. [sic] and he gave me no medicine or anything. It was on the Sunday that I saw the doctor. He gave me no satisfaction.' In the absence of a medical officer to confirm Morris's statement, the court made no attempt to adjourn the case for medical reports. Morris had to rely instead on the testimony of two character witnesses who stated he had been a willing worker, was of above average intelligence and had given no cause for trouble.[2]

As far as the British Army was concerned, desertion lowered the morale of the troops and punishment was harsh, especially in wartime. A soldier could be given the death sentence. Herbert was court-martialled and sentenced to be shot for desertion from active service. His death sentence was confirmed by Field Marshal Douglas Haig. Herbert was paraded in front of 6BWIR as an example. In the early hours of 20 September 1917 Herbert Morris dictated a letter to Padre Horner for his parents in Jamaica, and was executed at dawn by a firing squad that included seven West Indian and three white soldiers. He had just had his 17th birthday.

Chaplain Ramson recounted the events of the day of the execution:

At 5. a.m. we were on our way through the damp morning mist, and a drizzling rain [...] We were admitted at once to the cell, and again lifted up our hearts to God in earnest supplication for the condemned man. He was quite calm and told us he was prepared to die. The guard came; his hands were hand-cuffed behind his back: a thick cloth wrapped over his head, and a white cardboard disk pinned on his tunic over the heart: and he was marched out of the cell into the courtyard and tied securely to a post a few feet from the wall. On a small barricade of sandbags, some 20 paces off, were 10 rifles loaded, and with bolts drawn back ready for firing: one had a blank cartridge in it, as is customary, and no one of the firing party knew into which rifle it had been placed. While the prisoner was being secured to the post, the ten men, seven of whom were men of the BWIR and three white, were marched in and knelt behind the rifles: the attendants stepped back: the Captain raised his hand: aim was taken:

the Captain's hand dropped smartly, and the 10 rifles rang out as one shot. The body at the post gave one convulsive shudder and was still [...] Seven shots had passed through the heart and body into the wall behind, one through the neck, and one missed.[3]

Private Herbert Morris was buried in Belgium's Poperinge New Military Cemetery. Almost ninety years later, on 8 November 2006, he was pardoned along with 300 other soldiers who were executed for desertion and other offences during the First World War. Des Browne, the Defence Secretary, said of the move which does not quash or alter the convictions or sentences:

> This is not about rewriting history. I do not want to second guess decisions made by the commanders at the time. I believe it is better to acknowledge that injustices were clearly done in some cases – even if we cannot say which – and to acknowledge that all these men were victims of war.[4]

There is a document in the National Archives that is signed by the Secretary of State for Defence and confirms that Herbert 'is pardoned under Section 359 of the Armed Forces Act 2006. The pardon stands as recognition that he was one of many victims of the First World War and that execution was not a fate he deserved.'

Notes

1. Richard Smith, *Jamaican Volunteers in the First World War: Race, Masculinity and the Development of National Consciousness* (Manchester University Press, 2004), p. 84.
2. Ibid.
3. J. Ramson, *Carry On: Or Pages from the life of a West Indian Padre in the Field* (Jamaica: The Educational Supply Co., 1918) quoted in Glenford Howe, *Race, War and Nationalism: A Social History of West Indians in the First World War* (Ian Randle, 2002), pp. 156–57.
4. Richard Norton-Taylor, 'Pardons for executed soldiers become law', *Guardian*, 9 November 2006.

7

A BLACK TOMMY AT
THE SOMME

On 22 May 2009 the *Independent* published a feature-length article by John Lichfield about a treasure trove of First World War photographs that had been discovered in France. Lichfield says: 'Most First World War photographs show smart soldiers during or just after combat. Here we see the clear and often modern-looking features of soldiers at rest, either before – or in some cases, it seems – just after fighting in the trenches.' The collection of almost 400 images depicted British soldiers on the eve of, and during, the Battle of the Somme in 1916. Hundreds of thousands of British soldiers and their comrades from across the empire were preparing for 'The Big Push', the biggest British offensive of the war so far. The photographs had been preserved on glass plates, but they remained undisturbed in the attic of an old barn situated 10 miles behind the battlefields of the Somme until 2007. That year, when the barn changed ownership, the glass plates were thrown out, but passers-by started to collect some of them and eventually their significance and historical value began to be appreciated and acknowledged. Regrettably some of the plates were damaged, but others remained in perfect condition.

It is believed that the photos were taken in the winter of 1915–16 and the spring/summer of 1916 by an amateur photographer, possibly a local farmer who saw the opportunity to make a few francs. His name is not known, but he may have been supplementing his income by charging British soldiers for photos which they could send home to their families and sweethearts. Undoubtedly the photographs would have found their way to Britain or Australia or New Zealand. In some of the photographs the Tommies are shown in front of the same battered door or in a pear and apple orchard. Says John Lichfield: 'Within a few months – or days, most probably – many of the soldiers were dead.' He describes the 'somewhere in France' location where the pictures were taken as a village called Warloy-Baillon in the area known as the Somme. This was just 10 miles to the east of front line 'from which the British Army launched the most murderous battle of that, or any, war, which lasted from 1 July to late November 1916 and killed an estimated 1,000,000 British Empire, French and German soldiers.'[2] Warloy-Baillon was the site of a large hospital, taken over by the British Army.

John Lichfield says that the photographs:

Form a poignant record of the British Army on the eve of, or during, the Battle of the Somme: the smiling, the scared, the scruffy, the smart, the formal, the jokey, the short, the tall, the young and the old. There is even an image of a 1914–18 war phenomenon which was rarely photographed and scarcely ever mentioned: a black Tommy in artillery uniform, with two white comrades.[3]

The 'black Tommy' is seen standing with his left hand resting on the shoulder of one of his white comrades who is sitting down. The three Tommies look exhausted. Michael Stedman, a historian of the British during the First World War, has identified them as members of the Royal Regiment of Artillery or Royal Garrison Artillery. Stedman said:

Look at the chalk dust on their boots and general cleanliness of their kit. Chalk dust only arose in the summer campaigning on the 1916 Somme battlefield as the terrain dried out. My bet is that this photo was taken in the summer of 1916 (probably August/September). The men look worn, gaunt, frayed and very fit and lean, from relatively little food and an open air existence. I suspect they have been in action for some time [...] They are clearly friends – hands on shoulders and all that.[4]

The photographs have survived because of two local men: Bernard Gardin, a photography enthusiast, and Dominique Zanardi, the proprietor of the 'Tommy' cafe at Pozieres, a village in the heart of the Somme battlefields. Gardin was given a batch of about 270 glass plates and he approached Zanardi, a collector of First World War memorabilia, who had collected 130 similar plates from local people. Prints were made, at their own expense, from the original plates and many of the images turned out to be excellent. Gardin scanned the damaged plates into a computer and digitally restored the images. Prints of more than a hundred of the unknown soldiers have now been framed and exhibited in Zanardi's cafe in Pozières, although sadly the identity of the photographer remains unknown. Says Zanardi: 'My belief is that he lived close to the barn where the plates were found. He may have been a farmer. The plates were just stacked up after he printed photographs from them and then forgotten for more than ninety years.' Gardin adds: 'We think they form an important, and moving, historical record. Our motive in restoring them was not financial. It was a tribute to all the British soldiers who fought here and also to an unknown photographer.'[5]

Notes

1. John Lichfield, 'The unseen photographs that throw new light on the First World War', *Independent*, 22 May 2009.
2. Ibid.
3. Ibid.
4. The Poor Mouth: A Black Tommy at the Somme, http://thepoormouth.blogspot. co.uk/2009/05/black-tommy-at-somme.html
5. Lichfield, *Independent*.

8

SEAFORD CEMETERY

On the south-east coast of England, in a place called Seaford in Sussex, there is a cemetery. Seaford is close to the harbour and wartime embarkation post of Newhaven, and the town cemetery, on the road to the east, was opened in 1897. There are 253 First World War graves there (tended by the Commonwealth War Graves Commission), 189 being Canadian. Nineteen of the headstones display the crest of the British West Indies Regiment (BWIR). They mark the graves of army recruits who had travelled from the West Indies to Seaford; all of them died at the Seaford training camp between 20 October 1915 and 30 January 1916. However, it took until the 1990s for them to be remembered and commemorated, and for members of their families to be located and invited to the cemetery.

The nineteen soldiers had come from as far afield as Jamaica, St Lucia, British Guiana (Guyana), British Honduras (Belize) and Barbados. They all died during the winter of 1915–16 from mumps, pneumonia or influenza because the majority of these soldiers faced a hostile climate when they arrived at the camp. The terrible conditions had led to protests as early as October 1915. In his unpublished memoir of the BWIR, Lieutenant Colonel Charles Wood-Hill described what the soldiers faced when they arrived in Seaford:

The winter in England, especially to men from the Tropics, made serious training quite impossible. The men were housed in huts, which in summer time might have proved suitable, but in winter, when there was so much rain and damp – and the huts themselves hastily knocked up, as admissions to hospital proved, these huts were almost death-traps. The sickness was so terrible that the hospitals in the locality were filled to overflowing and the entire life and training of these two Battalions paralysed thereby.[1]

He was not alone in complaining about the conditions at the training camp in Seaford. As early as October 1915 Henry Somerset, a Guyanese ex-policeman and engineer, and other 'ringleaders' from Trinidad, protested about the terrible conditions at the camp, and were promptly sent back home.[2]

In *The Great Silence: 1918–1920 Living in the Shadow of the Great War* (2010), Juliet Nicolson has acknowledged that the soldiers found a more welcoming climate outside the Seaford training camp:

The local inhabitants of Seaford found the men congenial and in December 1915 the *Eastbourne Chronicle* had reported that at a church service held by the Bishop of Lewes, fifty-three West Indian soldiers had come forward to be confirmed. 'It was inspiring to see the reverent attitude of the soldiers,' the paper observed, 'who being 4,000 miles from home, discharged their duty to the Empire and found a welcome in the mother church.' To make the occasion even more pleasurable, the Seaford branch of the Ancient Order of Foresters, discovering that some of the visiting soldiers were members of the same organisation, arranged for them all to pose together in a joint photograph.[3]

In 1994 the first memorial service for the nineteen soldiers of the BWIR was held at the cemetery in Seaford. It was attended by members of the London-based West Indian Ex-Services Association. In 2006, members of the families of some of the soldiers travelled from the West Indies to visit the graves. The gravestone of an 18-year-old Jamaican, Private Harold Constantine Grubb, who died on 13 December 1915, has had a few words added by surviving relatives: 'Sacred to thy memory. Died for King and country.'[4] War cemeteries in Belgium and France have graves of BWIR soldiers also, as well as West Derby (Liverpool) and the Efford Cemetery in Plymouth, which has more than a dozen BWIR graves among the 338 from the First World War.

Notes

1. Lieutenant Colonel Charles Wood-Hill, 'A Few Notes on the History of the British West Indies Regiment', unpublished, 1919, p. 2.
2. For further information see Glenford Howe, *Race, War and Nationalism: A Social History of West Indians in the First World War* (Ian Randle, 2002), pp. 92–93.
3. Juliet Nicolson, *The Great Silence: 1918–1920 Living in the Shadow of the Great War* (John Murray, 2010), p. 163.
4. See '1915 – West Indian Men in Sussex' on the Brighton and Hove Black History site www.black-history.org.uk/westindies.asp.

9

'THOU SHALT NOT KILL'

Dr Alfred Salter (1873–1945) was a British medical practitioner and Labour Party politician who, as a pacifist, was a strong opponent of the First World War. On 24 September 1914 he wrote in the *Labour Leader*: 'I believe that all killing is murder and is wrong'. He then published a pamphlet which he called *Faith of a Pacifist*, which sold over a million copies. Salter joined the Non-Conscription Fellowship (NCF), an organisation formed by two pacifists, Clifford Allen and Fenner Brockway. The NCF encouraged men to refuse war service and required its members to 'refuse from conscientious motives to bear arms because they consider human life to be sacred'. In south-east London, Salter formed the Bermondsey branch of the NCF. After making several anti-war speeches a local newspaper posed the question: 'Is Dr. Salter Pro-German?' However, several of his patients sent letters to the newspaper in which they defended their doctor. His biographer, Fenner Brockway, later explained in *Bermondsey Story: The Life of Alfred Salter* (1949) that the working-class people of Bermondsey respected Salter as a man and a doctor rather than as a pacifist.

During the First World War Joan Fry, a Quaker visitor to Pentonville Prison, reported to the NCF the case of Isaac Hall, a black conscientious objector. Salter went to see him. At the prison he befriended Isaac, who was extremely tall (6ft 6½in). He was the grandchild of a slave on a sugar plantation in Jamaica. A skilled carpenter, he had travelled to Britain just before the outbreak of war when he was 35 years old, and was employed making shop counters for Messrs Lyons. He tried to return to Jamaica when war was declared, but could not secure a passage. In 1916, when conscription was introduced, Isaac was ordered to report for military service, but he held strong Christian beliefs, and believed in the commandment 'Thou shalt not kill'. He went before a tribunal as a conscientious objector. In *Bermondsey Story* Fenner Brockway states that Isaac was told that he was an 'ignorant, unlettered creature who had no right to any opinions' and describes what happened next:

> He did not report to the military and was arrested. He was taken to a training camp and, on refusing to obey an order to fall in and quick march, was dragged round the parade ground face downwards until he was unconscious. Then he was court-martialled and sentenced to two years' hard labour. At Pentonville Prison he was ordered to do work on soldiers' haversacks. When he refused he was placed in solitary confinement and on bread and water diet. On completing his punishment he was ordered to do the same work. He refused; more punishment followed. This experience was repeated again and again. In time this giant Negro [...] became wasted to a shadow. He contracted a cough and could hardly stand. The prison doctor feared that he might be developing consumption and that he might collapse and die. It was at this point that Dr. Salter visited him.[1]

Dr Salter was horrified at the sight of Isaac, who had become a living skeleton. He came face to face with a gaunt, bent, starved and broken man. One of the prison warders told Salter that Isaac was the bravest man he had ever encountered. Salter then informed one of the Under-Secretaries for War at Whitehall about Isaac's condition, and the Minister expressed his shock at Salter's description of Isaac: 'If half of what you have told me is true, it makes me ashamed of being an Englishman.' Two days later Dr Salter received a telegram that orders had been given for Isaac's release. He took a taxi to the prison, brought him to his home in Storks Road, Bermondsey, and there Isaac was given shelter and nursed back to health for nine months until a passage to the West Indies could be secured.

Notes

1. Fenner Brockway, *Bermondsey Story: The Life of Alfred Salter* (George Allen and Unwin, 1949), pp. 67–68.

10

WILLIAM ROBINSON CLARKE: A WING AND A PRAYER

After the outbreak of the war, the Jamaican-born Manley brothers, Norman and Roy (see Chapter 4), considered enlisting in the Royal Flying Corps before they joined the army. Norman recalled:

> It had already become clear that the aeroplane would play an important role [...] the air, so far as England was concerned, was a new and unde-veloped thing. Training schools were to a large extent privately operated under special contracts with the British Government, so we were told that if we could find £150 each, we could get into such a school and if we qualified in six months and earned flying certificates, we would be con-sidered for admission. I did not have that money.[1]

As Norman Manley predicted, the First World War saw the emer-gence of the aeroplane as an instrument of war. It also gave opportunities to a small number of 'men of colour' to become flying pioneers. These included several Indian nationals who were com-missioned into the Royal Flying Corps which, from 1 April 1918, was known as the Royal Air Force. They served on the Western and Italian Fronts. One such volunteer was Lieutenant Indra Lal 'Laddie' Roy, who served as a fighter pilot with Nos 56 and 40 Squadrons on the Western Front during 1917–18. Prior to his death in action on 22 July 1918, 'Laddie' was involved in the destruction of ten enemy aircraft, and became India's first fighter 'ace'. In recognition of his gallantry and skill, he was posthumously awarded the Distinguished Flying Cross (DFC) in September 1918. Other non-whites who became flying pioneers at this time included Eugene Bullard, the first African American to be recognised as a military pilot. Bullard moved to Paris and, at the start of the First World War, he joined the French Foreign Legion. Wounded at the bloody and horrific Battle of Verdun in 1916, and a recipient of the Croix de Guerre, he then joined the Lafayette Flying Corps in 1917 and flew twenty combat missions, claiming two kills. He was known as 'The Black Swallow of Death'. As soon as America entered the war in April 1917, Bullard volunteered for service in the US Army Air Service, but he was rejected on the basis of his race. Ignored in his homeland, Bullard was better remembered in France and in 1954 the French government invited him to help rekindle the everlasting flame at the Tomb of the Unknown Soldier under the Arc de Triomphe in Paris. Then in 1959 he was made a Chevalier of the Légion d'honneur, France's highest decoration. He died in obscurity in 1961, a stranger in his own country, America, having been badly beaten and permanently injured in a racist attack in New York in 1949.

It took time for William Robinson Clarke to be recognised as one of the first West Indian pilots who flew for Britain in the First World War. 'Robbie' Clarke was born in Kingston, Jamaica in 1895 to Egbert James Clarke and Eugenia Sarah née Cohen. On 29 June 1915 Jamaica's newspaper *The Gleaner* reported on the young man's interest in automobiles, and his departure to England to support the war effort:

Ever since he left school the young man has worked sturdily to make himself master of the intricacies of the engines of the automobiles and other motor vehicles, and the success with which his efforts have been attended is marked by the many difficult pieces of work that he has put through. The position of affairs in England today leads one to confidently state that such workers as Mr. Clarke are the men who will be very useful in Lord Kitchener's organization. He is full of energy and is hard as nails. Mr. Clarke has a distinct leaning to aircraft work, and should he succeed in getting behind 'the wheel', we feel sure that in the hour of danger he will not lack the courage and pluck which are the parents of brave deeds. He carries with him quite a little stock of letters of recommendation from professional men and motor experts of the city.[2]

Now and again Robbie sent accounts of his exploits in France to *The Gleaner*. The following was published on 7 September 1917:

> Things were very hot when I was in France. Oh! The suffering the fellows have to bear. It is indescribable. I got my 'packet' over the Ypres front about five miles on the German side. I was photographing, and after taking the photos, was looking out for a nice place to give Fritz a couple of pills (bombs). We were so taken up looking for a good target, that we forgot to look out for enemy scouts. The first thing I knew was hearing the rat-a-tat-tat of his machine guns, and glancing back, saw about five of them diving for me, and I could not get away in time. I was hit almost at the start of the scrap. The machine was riddled. A very uncommon, though not unusual, thing happened just previously. One of our shells passed right between our planes. Both observer and myself heard it touch one of the wires. Thank goodness it did not touch the engine. When I was hit I was about 5,000 feet up. It was my second scrap and I fared worse than the first one. We are not quite sure, but we believe we did get one in the first scrap which took place a couple of days before, as we saw him go down as though he was hit.[3]

When Robbie died in 1981, A.S. Phillips, Professor at the University of the West Indies, paid tribute to him at his funeral and described some of his achievements:

> I may say that Robbie Clarke's exploits as a flyer may justly be termed legendary. I remember my awe and admiration when I discovered that he actually flew with the Royal Flying Corps, the predecessor of the Royal Air Force. I have recently learnt that he was the first Jamaican and the first West Indian ever to gain Pilots Wings in this branch of the British Fighting Services. Indeed it is claimed, that he was the 208th Service Pilot in the entire British Commonwealth. The episode in 1917 in which Pilot Clarke while on an operational flight was attacked by German fighters in the air, and though severely wounded, nevertheless managed to fly his R.E.8 aeroplane back to a relatively safe crash-landing behind the allied lines, places him in that special category of the genuine war hero.[4]

In 2008 'Robbie' Clarke was included in the Imperial War Museum's *From War to Windrush* exhibition, and in 2013 the Royal Air Force Museum featured him in their 'Pilots of the Caribbean' exhibition.

Peter Devitt, Curator in the Archives Division of the Royal Air Force Museum, confirms that an unknown number of black personnel did serve in Britain's flying services (Royal Flying Corps, Royal Naval Air Service and Royal Air Force) during the First World War:

> But we didn't know until a few years ago that there had been a black pilot flying for Britain. He was William Robinson Clarke from Kingston, Jamaica who, in 1915, paid his own passage to come to Britain and joined the Royal Flying Corps. He qualified as a pilot on 26 April 1917, and we know this because the museum holds the Royal Aero Club's archive which includes albums of photographs of all those that passed the Royal Aero Club pilot's test and won their 'wings'. We didn't know about 'Robbie' Clarke until a volunteer working for the Royal Aero Club came out of the archive holding one of the photo albums and there was a black face. We were then able to research Sergeant Clarke's career and learned that he flew RE8 biplanes over the Western Front with No. 4 Squadron RFC in the summer of 1917. We also found out that on 28 July that year his aircraft had been attacked by five enemy fighters and he'd been shot down and wounded – we have his Casualty Card in our collection. Happily, William Robinson Clarke recovered from his wounds and returned to Jamaica, living a long and happy life and passing away in April 1981. We didn't know that there had been a black pilot and it made us aware that there is so much research to be done on the subject of black personnel in the RAF over time.[5]

Notes

1. Norman Manley, 'The Autobiography of Norman Washington Manley', *Jamaica Journal*, vol. 7, no. 1–2 (March–June 1973), p. 6.
2. 'Young Jamaican Volunteers for Lord Kitchener's Great Army', *The Gleaner*, 29 June 1915. With thanks to Andrew Dawrant and The Royal Aero Club.
3. 'Flyer Wounded: Young Jamaica Airman Attacked by Several German Scouts. Though in Great Pain, Pilots Machine Back To British Lines', *The Gleaner*, 7 September 1917. With thanks to Andrew Dawrant and The Royal Aero Club.
4. Thanks to Andrew Dawrant and The Royal Aero Trust for providing this information.
5. Peter Devitt, interview with Stephen Bourne, London, 3 November 2013.

PART II:

THE HOME FRONT

11

AN AFRICAN IN TRURO

In *The Bells of Truro* (1994) Phyllis M. Jones locates the Cornish city of Truro 'between the Atlantic and the English Channel'. She says it was sited at the head of the Truro River:

> But long since the water has been pushed back by the flow of silt from the many small rivers, which have run down from the hills and there is now a car park where once the masts of ships were seen at Lemon Quay. The River Fal is wide, a tidal river with green woods on either side, and it spreads into glossy, shadowed creeks as it reaches Falmouth Harbour.[1]

It was in this idyllic Cornish location that an African seaman made his home and raised a family. He had been born in Ghana on 23 December 1868, the son of James and Sheshaboo Equaggo, but he was given the name John Cockle by the captain of one of his ships. After he had learned to read and write, John decided to add his African family name of Equaggo.

On 20 November 1911, in Great Yarmouth, at the age of 42, John married a white British woman, Elizabeth Vincent. On his marriage certificate John described his father as a Chief from the West Coast of Africa. John and Elizabeth's first son, John Harrison Cockle, was born in Truro in 1912. Truro remained the family home all through the 1910s, during which time two more sons, Willie (1913) and Victor (1917) were born. John Sr continued to work as a merchant seaman, and Phyllis M. Jones remembers the family with great affection in *The Bells of Truro*. Phyllis includes them among the many neighbours she missed when her family moved away:

> We lost contact with the neighbours in Fairmantle Street, especially a coloured family, Mrs Cockle and her five sons [...] Mr Cockle was a seaman and was away most of the time on his ship and the boys, Harrison [aka John], William, Victor, George and Emmanuel, were accepted without question in the city of Truro. Mrs Cockle, Mother said, was a lady. If they knew just how much their memory lingered in my mother's so many years later! How they came in one Christmas when we lived in Fairmantle Street to listen to *Messiah* being played on an old gramophone with a trumpet in the front room. And how, during her last months, Mother would say, 'Now, then, let me run through the boys, the Cockles again. Let me see , Harrison, Willy, Victor, George and Emmanuel.[2]

John Cockle Sr was remembered with great affection by members of the local community. At John Jr's funeral in 1998, Bert Biscoe, a local councillor, told the congregation that he had 'found love, work and warm support in his early years in Truro'. Some years earlier the memories of Fred L. Piper included the following:

> John Cockle's father, I can see him now, down the street [Truro city centre] with Captain Didham, playing duet on the concertina. And as we knew Mr Cockle in those days, he used to go to sea. He was a lovely bloke. I don't think I've heard a word said against him. Every time he came home he was in the local Salvation Army. On Saturday nights they used to go down town by the Corn Exchange [formerly in Boscawen Street, Truro, on the site of the present British Home Stores].[3]

When BBC Radio Cornwall's presenter Chris Blount interviewed John Harrison Cockle Jr, he described how his father left Africa and settled in Truro:

> George Henry Harrison, a man for whom I'm named, was a young man who was serving his time as a ship's captain and he met my grandfather who was a Chief and a trader on the Gold Coast of West Africa. Grandfather and Captain Harrison got along very well. The old man was sent by his father down to the beach because there was no ports in

those days and as a boy of ten, we believe, or a bit more, he was sent with a parcel to take to the ship, the Flower of the Plate, which was George Henry Harrison's command, and he said 'Come aboard the ship, boy' and of course little black boys are the same as little white boys, he did everything he was told, and he had the chance to go on board a ship, and he was intrigued. The steward gave him rice pudding, so he was introduced to new foods. Anyhow, after he filled his little tummy, he lay down and went to sleep. Next thing he heard a lot of things going on, men shouting and the clank, clank, clank of the anchor coming in, and they were making sail. He told us many many times how, as a little boy, he looked over and saw his native land disappearing. His mother hadn't been told about it. Nobody knew where he was. He disappeared.[4]

The young West African was given the name 'John Cockle' because someone of that name who was listed in the ship's register was no longer aboard:

Anyway, he went down to South America, amongst other places. He ended up in Brazil where he was sold and joined a British ship and eventually he came to Liverpool. He was a very fortunate little man because he was sold, but he was well loved. He loved people and people loved him. Liverpool was a great port in those days. All those docks up there. All the people coming into the port of Liverpool. The ships that were carrying cargoes. My father came ashore as a little boy but he didn't like Liverpool. Too many people there. Too much rushing and tearing around. He was a quiet little boy. He had a shilling in his pocket and he walked down to Garston and he picked up a little bag somewhere and he walked back from Garston. He met a man on the road: 'Where you going, boy?' Dad told us he sounded like a West Country man because as a result of meeting this man he joined a schooner belonging to a John Farley of Looe. John Cockle Senior eventually arrived in Looe where a strange face, especially a black face, was unique, and he married there. But his wife, and their baby, died. If you go to St Martin's Churchyard in Looe, you will find a gravestone which says 'Sacred to the memory of Sophia Equaggo Cockle. Beloved wife of John Equaggo Cockle.' And their child was also buried in the same grave.[5]

John married his first wife Sophia Batten in 1889 and their daughter Jane Sophia was born in 1890. Neither John's wife nor daughter survived, dying during the summer of 1890, probably from tuberculosis. During the West Country's great blizzard of March 1891, John played the accordion and sang hymns to entertain the occupants of a railway carriage when they were snowed up. Says John Jr:

Dad came to Truro about the same time they were building the cathedral. He liked Truro and he was a good man. He wanted a quiet life. And he got a quiet life and people would take him to chapel or the Salvation Army. In 1896 he had a house in Chapel Hill. Eventually he met our mother through the ranks of the Salvation Army. He was a keen Salvationist, and she was a Junior Sergeant Major. But she was a noisy little thing and she wanted to save his soul for Jesus. It wasn't love at first sight. She fell in love with him afterwards. They married in Yarmouth and he brought her down to Truro. Poor soul. She had a rough time in Great Yarmouth where they were married. Her relatives were not very nice to her, especially when they knew she was going out with a black man. It caused a stir in Truro because mother was a character and she stood by her children through thick and thin.

My mother and father were strict religious people. Our mother was a wonderful lady. She was a little woman. 4ft 11in. Mother had very keen ideas regarding religion. Our mother used to preach in Victoria Square on Saturday night. Father was not so keen on it. But mother was a terror with it. There would be a big crowd around them. You could walk on their heads. The Salvation Army would have an evening open-air service and if our father was home from the sea he would be there playing his concertina and singing and everyone was intrigued to see a little black man singing and he had a stutter and it intrigued people but once he got into full flood you couldn't stop him. And he went to Newquay preaching. Both my parents preached, and my father played the concertina, the violin and sang. I would say he was known throughout the world, Johnny Cockle, black man, seaman. He always worked. It didn't matter what kind of ship it was. He had the ability and the guts to get along with a crowd of men on a ship in the days when they had no respect for one another: 'Hang on a minute, Johnny's gonna pray.' And every evening they would stop everything when father got on his knees by the side of his bunk and prayed. He was well known for that.[6]

John Cockle Sr died at the age of 86 years on 29 May 1955 and the following obituary was published in the *West Briton* newspaper on 2 June 1955:

Son of Chief James Equaggo, one of the few African paramount chiefs to attend in state the Coronation of Queen Victoria [Westminster Abbey, 28 June 1838], Mr. John Equaggo-Cockle, of 60 Fairmantle Street, Truro, died on Sunday at Budock Hospital, Falmouth. His age is given as 87, but members of his family believe him to be considerably older. Bearing the family name of Equaggo, he was a member of the Ifri tribe of the Gold Coast, British West Africa, and was related to the Hon. Kwame Nkrumah, the present Prime Minister of the Colony. Many members of his tribe hold high administrative positions in West Africa.

Brought to England at an early age in the barquentine *La Flore de la Plate*, Mr Cockle as he later became known came ashore at the Custom House at Falmouth, and it will be from this spot that his ashes will be taken out into the Bay and scattered on the sea on Monday morning from the launch Pathfinder, owned by his eldest son, Mr John Cockle, of Truro.

Mr Cockle was not able to attend school in England, but he went to sea when quite young and soon learned to read and write, and he was able to discourse on many subjects. He assumed the surname Cockle after he joined his first ship. The captain, unable to pronounce his full tribal names, said jocularly 'Call him Cockle, after the cabin boy who jumped the ship last voyage.' And Cockle he was known hereafter. He served in the foreign and coastal trade in British ships until 1933 and was an early member of the original Seamen's Union, founded by Mr Havelock Wilson.

Of deep religious convictions, Mr Cockle had been a member of the Salvation Army since 1885 and is believed to have been the first emigrant from the Gold Coast to return there as a disciple of 'the Army' which is now very strong in the colony [...] although he had been blind for 18 years, he was until about five years ago a familiar figure at the Saturday night 'Army' gatherings in Boscawen Street, Truro.[7]

John Cockle Jr said that, when he was a child, he did not know what it was to be black until the day his mother was wheeling him and his brother Willie along St Nicholas Street in a pushchair:

I remember, on a high summer's day, I would say about 1915 or 1916, a tall gawky boy said to a woman who was with him, 'Oh, Ma, black boys!' I said to my mother, 'Ma, he said black boys.' And she laid into him firmly. And his mother, who was a gawky, ignorant-looking woman, said 'Aren't they lovely. Handsome.' And my mother said, 'You go away and leave my children alone.' I realised then I was different from everyone else because

I didn't know what black boy meant (laughs). We've had these problems from time to time. Nothing serious. Truro is my city. Every stick and stone is mine. I regard Truro as a beautiful little place. Like heaven.[8]

Bert Biscoe remembered John Cockle Jr (1912–98) as 'an eloquent, defiant and proud Cornishman and was welcomed as such, with equal pride, by Cornish people, along with his brothers, parents and subsequent generations'.

Notes

1. Phyllis M. Jones, *The Bells of Truro* (Landfall Publications, 1994), p. 15.
2. Ibid., pp. 72–73.
3. Unpublished transcript of an interview with Fred L. Piper in 1987 held by the Courtney Library and Cornish History Research Centre (Truro).
4. Chris Blount, interview with John Cockle (1990s). Thanks to Chris Blount for sharing this.
5. Ibid.
6. Ibid.
7. With thanks to Kim Cooper, Principal Library Officer, Cornish Studies Library, for providing information about John Cockle Sr.
8. Chris Blount.

Left: Lionel Turpin. (Jackie Turpin and W. Terry Fox, *Battling Jack: You Gotta Fight Back*, Mainstream Publishing, 2005)

Below: Walter Tull. (Courtesy of the Finlayson Family Archive)

Above left: Alhaji Grunshi of the Gold Coast Regiment, who on 12 August 1914 fired the first shot for Britain in the First World War.

Above: Albert and Ethel James, Liverpool. (Courtesy of Ray Costello)

Left: Private Harold Brown (Royal West Surrey Regiment). (Courtesy of the Imperial War Museum MISC 2816-5579-5)

Marcus Bailey (standing) and an unidentified soldier. (Courtesy of Lilian Bader and Adrian Bader)

British West Indies Regiment at Seaford Camp in February 1916 with their officer, Lieutenant Charles Paul. (Courtesy of John Paul)

British West Indies Regiment stacking 8in shells with Australian troops, Ypres, October 1917. (Courtesy of the Imperial War Museum E2078)

South African Native Labour Corps. (Courtesy of the Imperial War Museum Q2382)

King George V inspecting representatives of the South African Native Labour Corps at Abbeville, 9 June 1917. (Courtesy of the Imperial War Museum Q2573)

16. RUN AWAY, KAISER WILLIAM

Patriotic song at the end of the First World War.

Run Away, Kaiser William. Patriotic Trinidadian calypso from the First World War. Edric Connor, editor, *Songs from Trinidad* (Oxford University Press, 1958).

Major General Sir E.W. Chaytor decorating officers and men of the 1st and 2nd British West Indies Regiment in 1918. The recipient is believed to be the Trinidadian 661 Lance Corporal McCollin Leekam. (Frank Cundall, *Jamaica's Part in the Great War 1914–1918*, 1925, and www.blackpresence.co.uk)

British West Indies Regiment in Palestine (1917). (Courtesy of John Paul)

Above left: The final resting place of Private Herbert Norris of the British West Indies Regiment, Poperinge New Military Cemetery, Belgium. Norris was executed on 20 September 1917 and pardoned in 2006. (Courtesy of The War Graves Photographic Project in association with the Commonwealth War Graves Commission)

Above: The final resting place of Private Harold C. Grubb of the British West Indies Regiment, Seaford Cemetery. He died in Seaford on 13 December 1915, aged 18. (Courtesy of Jeffrey Green)

Left: William Robinson Clarke. (Courtesy of The Royal Aero Club)

John Equaggo Cockle.
(Sheila Bird, *Bygone Truro*
Phillimore, 1986)

Esther and Joseph Bruce,
London, 1918. (Author's
collection)

Stephen Bourne and his adopted aunt, Esther Bruce, born in London before the First World War, with Joan Caruana, Mayor of Hammersmith and Fulham, at the launch of *Aunt Esther's Story*, 1991. (Author's collection)

Mabel Mercer with Clinton Rosemond and John Payne, 1920s. (Author's collection)

Scott and Whaley. (Author's collection)

Belle Davis. (Courtesy of Rainer Lotz)

Left: Amanda Ira Aldridge and (inset) Ira Aldridge. (Author's collection)

Below: 'Racial Riots at Cardiff', *Western Mail*, 14 June 1919. The 'man of colour' referred to in the caption is Dr Rufus Fennell. (Courtesy of Cardiff Libraries/Media Wales Ltd)

WESTERN MAIL. SATURDAY, JUNE 14, 1919.

RACIAL RIOTS AT CARDIFF.

A " man of colour " addressing a crowd in the Tiger Bay district on Friday. He advised his countrymen to do nothing likely to cause trouble.　　　　　　　　　　[Western Mail photo.

Above: The Coloured Men's Institute's outing from London's East End to Reigate (1926); Kamal Chunchie can be seen in the centre. (Reproduced with the kind permission of Mrs Anita Bowes and the Cozier family)

Left: Avril Coleridge-Taylor and (inset) Samuel Coleridge-Taylor. (Author's collection)

DR. FENNELL.

Left: Dr Rufus Fennell, *Western Mail*, 19 July 1919. (Courtesy of Cardiff Libraries/Media Wales Ltd)

Below: Dr Harold Moody Park in Nunhead, London SE15 and (inset) Dr Harold Moody. (Courtesy of Tim Otway)

Above: Evelyn Dove. (Author's collection)

Left: John Archer. (Wandsworth Borough Council)

Left: A black Tommy at the Somme. (Courtesy of Bernard Gardin and Dominique Zanardi)

Below: American soldiers at a basketball match in Hyde Park, London, 1918. (Author's collection)

12

THE TWO JOSEPHINES

Shortly before the outbreak of the First World War, two mixed-race girls were born in London and given the same forename: Josephine. Their fathers, Joseph Bruce and Napoleon Florent, had similar backgrounds. As seamen, they had travelled to the mother country from different parts of the British Empire and settled in the metropolis in the Edwardian era. They married white British women and, during the First World War, to help support their families, they both found steady employment in an extravagant London musical production called *Chu Chin Chow*. It was based on the story of *Ali Baba and the Forty Thieves* and it premiered at His Majesty's Theatre on 3 August 1916. The show ran for a record-breaking five years with 2,238 performances and provided regular work – and a steady income – for many black men in wartime Britain. They were employed to add a touch of exotic 'colour' to the production in non-speaking roles as extras. Theatre audiences flocked to see this spectacle, and these included soldiers and sailors on leave from the armed services who appreciated this entertaining diversion from the horrors and stresses of the First World War. One member of the audience who never forgot the experience was a young schoolboy called John Gielgud. He later found fame on the stage as one of Britain's most celebrated actors. Gielgud's biographer, Jonathan Croall, commented: 'With *Chu Chin Chow*, which he was to see a dozen times, he was moved less by the acting and music than by the scenery and costumes, the real goats, sheep and camels, the mysterious caves and gorgeous palaces.'' There is no evidence that the fathers of the two Josephines ever met, but their parallel lives in Britain during the First World War are not untypical of most British bi-racial families at that time.

Josephine was the real name of Esther Bruce, but throughout her life she was known to her family as Esther, and to her friends as Josie. When Esther came into this world at 15 Dieppe Street, Fulham, on 29 November 1912, King George V was the reigning monarch and the Liberal H.H. Asquith was Prime Minister. By the time Esther was born, 1912 had been an eventful year: the British polar explorer Robert Falcon Scott and his team reached the South Pole, only to find that Amundsen had beaten them to it; suffragettes smashed shop windows in London's West End; the 'unsinkable' White Star liner RMS *Titanic* struck an iceberg and sank on her maiden voyage from the United Kingdom to New York; and the tradition of the Blackpool illuminations began. On 1 September, just three months before Esther was born, another black Briton, the celebrated Croydon-born composer Samuel Coleridge-Taylor, died at the age of 37. Just three weeks short of Esther's first birthday, another black Briton made history. This was John Archer, who, on 10 November 1913, was elected as Mayor of Battersea in 1913 by 40 votes to 39. He thus became the first person of African descent to hold civic office in London.

Esther's father, Joseph Bruce, had travelled to Britain in the Edwardian era from Guyana, then a crown colony which was known as British Guiana. He was an early black settler in Britain and he came at a time when there were very few black people there apart from the small but growing working-class black communities who were thriving in various seaports like Cardiff, Liverpool and Canning Town in the East End of London. Esther explained:

> Dad didn't talk much about his life in British Guiana but he did tell me he was the son of John Bruce, a carpenter. He said his mother's name was Mary Ann Bruce and they were descended from slaves. Dad worked on the ships before he came to Britain. He told me he travelled about the world. It couldn't have been easy for him, because there weren't many black people here, but he was tough. He could look after himself.[2]

In the 1911 census, taken on 2 April, Joseph Bruce was recorded as a seaman, lodging in the dockland area of London's East End. He was a single man, age 30, from Demerara in British Guiana. He was boarding with seamen from Demerara and Grenada at 21 Crown Street,

Tidal Basin. The 1911 census also revealed that Esther's mother, Edith Brooks, a 21-year-old servant, was visiting a family in North End Road, Fulham. She had been born in Hoxton Old Town, East London, in 1889, and she was accompanied by her 2-year-old son, William. She recorded his place of birth as Victoria Docks. A birth certificate for William revealed that he was born illegitimately in 1908 in a home for unmarried mothers in Eldon Road, Tidal Basin. This was situated in the Victoria Docks area, close to where Joseph had lodgings in Crown Street. Therefore it is likely that Joseph met Edith here. Crown Street would later become the flashpoint for race riots towards the end of – and after – the First World War (1917 and 1919) when black citizens and bi-racial families came under attack (see Chapter 16) but Joseph and his family were not affected. His marriage to Edith had taken place in another part of London: Fulham, on 22 March 1912, and they made their home in the tight-knit working-class community of Dieppe Street, off North End Road. Joseph never returned to British Guiana. As a working-class man on a low income, it simply was not possible.

Though black people were rare in Fulham when Esther was born in 1912, Joseph did have a West Indian friend living nearby. Augustus Greenidge was not only a witness at Joseph and Edith's wedding, he also stood as Esther's godfather when she was christened in January 1913. Joseph was away from home when Esther was christened, but Edith describes the christening for him in a letter that has survived. It also reveals the close-knit, racially integrated community in which they lived: 'We had a lovely service on Sunday for Esther's christening. Everyone was so nice and made a great fuss of baby. Mr Stokly kept kissing her and saying what a pretty baby she was. Mr Murray gave a lovely address and prayed for you. Baby was very good indeed.'

Although Esther was born and raised in a predominantly white community, she never had a problem with her identity as a mixed-race child because her father was a proud and independent man. He instilled in his daughter a feeling of pride in being of African descent and he achieved this partly by informing her about some of the famous black people he had read about. These included Samuel Coleridge-Taylor and the African American boxing champion Jack Johnson. Joseph told Esther to remember she was as good as anyone else. Joseph always made a defiant stand against racism and retaliated against anyone who discriminated against him and his daughter (see Chapter 19).

From the age of 5 Esther went to school in North End Road, Fulham. She said she was not treated differently:

> We were all together. We had a teacher called Mrs. Carson. She was a funny old dear. One afternoon she said to the class: 'I'm going to teach you how to talk to people.' She taught us how to be polite to each other and then she said: 'Now, children, when you meet coloured people, you do not talk to them. Don't lower yourself. Don't forget, you do *not* talk to coloured people. Remember that.' When I went home Dad said: 'How did you get on at school today? What did you learn?' I ignored him. He said: 'What's wrong with you? Are you deaf?' I said: 'I was told at school not to speak to coloured people.' He said: 'Who told you that?' I said: 'Our teacher.' The next day Dad went to the school and raised the roof! Afterwards Mrs. Carson was sacked.[3]

Every Saturday night Joseph gave Esther and her brother Billy a treat. He took them to The Granville, a music hall in Fulham Broadway. Esther recalled:

> Inside it was beautiful. The carvings were really lovely. The dearest seats, which were downstairs and cost one shilling and sixpence, were red velvet, but we always sat upstairs in the gods, in the cheap seats. They were stone steps and cost fourpence. Four *old* pennies. We only sat downstairs if there was something big on, and then we felt honoured because we sat on proper seats. We bought a penny's worth of peanuts, or an orange. The big stage curtains were dark red and gold. There was an orchestra in the pit and as soon as they started to tune up we'd get excited and say: 'Here we go. They're gonna start.' It was always a variety show and lasted two hours. We saw all the great music hall stars. All the old ones like Max Miller, Nellie Wallace, and Hetty King. They were really classy people. Mind you, we were never allowed to go backstage and meet them, or ask them for autographs. We couldn't do anything like that. After the show we went home and baked some potatoes.

Another music hall star of the First World War period was the white entertainer G.H. Elliott who put on a black face and called himself 'The Chocolate Coloured Coon'. Esther saw him at The Granville, but as a young child Elliott's 'blacking up' did not offend her. She just enjoyed the entertainment. 'He sang his famous song "Lily of Laguna" and I thought he was great', she said.[4]

The First World War did not impact greatly on Esther. She recalled that her father did not join up. She remembered the time a Zeppelin appeared overhead and she went with her father and some of their neighbours onto West Kensington station (which was situated at the end of Dieppe Street) to have a look as it passed by. It must have been an unusual sight but thankfully it did not drop any bombs.

Esther did not recall much about the end of the First World War because her mother had been taken ill and died on 24 October 1918, just a few weeks before Armistice Day (11 November) and Esther's 6th birthday (29 November): 'I always remember we had horses in those days with black plumes and they were used for funerals. They pulled up outside our house in Dieppe Street and then the men put wreaths on the casket. Mother was buried in a coffin painted mauve.'[5]

Joseph Bruce was not a professional actor. His appearances in shows like *Chu Chin Chow* helped to supplement his main source of income as a builder's labourer. However, some black men of his generation, like Napoleon Florent, did pursue full-time careers as professional actors.

Florent was born on the island of Saint Lucia in the eastern Caribbean Sea in the 1870s. A captain of a ship was friendly with Napoleon's mother and he was chosen to travel with the captain who exported sugar and bananas from Saint Lucia. By the 1890s Napoleon was travelling the world as a seaman, and by 1901 he had settled in Britain. According to the 1901 census he was working as a member of George Sanger's circus in Grantham. He is listed as one of many circus labourers living in a tent in a cricket field. He gives his age as 26. In 1909 in London he married an Englishwoman, Frances Jewell Rouse, and they had eight children from 1910 to 1930. Josephine Jewell Florent was born on 5 July 1910 at 207 Hampstead Road (St Pancras). On the marriage and birth certificates Napoleon entered his profession as 'theatrical artiste' and 'actor' respectively. The Florents continued to live at 207 Hampstead Road throughout the First World War. Josephine remembered her father as 'A very stern man. He definitely had a Victorian attitude. That generation of West Indians were very strict.'[6]

From 1916 to 1921 *Chu Chin Chow* provided Napoleon with a regular source of income. However, Josephine recalled seeing him in an earlier West End show:

I remember being taken to see my father on the stage in *Kismet* at the Garrick Theatre in 1914. *Chu Chin Chow* soon followed and ran for five years. It kept my father in work for a very long time. I was a very small child at the time, but I do vividly remember seeing my father on stage in those productions wearing the most wonderful, exotic costumes. He didn't have speaking roles. He was an exotic extra in a harem. Off stage, father was a fine raconteur. To put it simply, if father got work in silent films, or on the stage, we ate. Father worked a lot in the early days, but by the time I was twelve, around 1922, the work dried up for several years. To help out financially, my mother went to work, even though she had a home and eight children to take care of. She worked all her life and could turn her hand to anything. I remember her working for a famous caterer. She made Christmas puddings for Australia and New Zealand. But mostly they were not very glamorous jobs.[7]

Josephine could just about remember the end of the war: 'I was 8 years old. It was a relief, especially for the mothers who were terrified they would lose their sons. We were glad the war was over but it was also a sad time because so many lives had been lost. Far too many.'[8]

In stark contrast to the relatively happy childhoods of the two Josephines, one of their contemporaries, Kathleen Wrsama, was treated cruelly. However, through sheer resilience and determination, the young girl survived. Kathleen was born in Ethiopia in East Africa in 1904 and was brought to England at the age of 2 by a church minister and his wife. They took the young child to live with them in Yorkshire, and were very strict. 'You daren't even breathe on a Sunday!' Kathleen later recalled. 'Although I called them 'Mother' and 'Father', I never really thought of them as my parents. I was frightened of them both. I didn't know who I was. I didn't know where I'd come from. They'd stolen my birthright.' They also stole her name, for it was not until she went to London as a young woman that she gave herself the name Kathleen. Until then she was known simply as 'Topsy'. She wasn't given a surname. She said: 'I knew that I was different and so I tried to get the colour off by scrubbing myself hard [...] all my mother could say was "What can you expect from a Heathen?"' Kathleen's foster parents died when she was about 7 and she was placed in an orphanage where she experienced even greater hostility and isolation. Kathleen was never allowed to mix with the forty other children. She was made to sleep alone in the attic. At 13 Kathleen ran away from the orphanage. A kind farmer and his wife took her in, and 'the farmer taught me to read and write, and he had a large library which he said I could help myself to'. At the age of 26 Kathleen left Yorkshire for the bright lights of London.[9]

After the First World War, Joseph Bruce continued to work as a builder's labourer and also as a film extra. He died in 1941 at the age of 60. Napoleon Florent continued working as a professional actor and bit-player in films until his final appearance in David Lean's *Oliver Twist* (1948). He died in 1959 at the age of 84. After leaving school Esther Bruce worked in service for a short time and then as a seamstress until she retired at the age of 74. In 1991 she co-authored her autobiography, *Aunt Esther's Story*, with her adopted nephew Stephen Bourne. Esther died in London in 1994 at the age of 81. Before the war Josephine Florent worked for a medical solicitor, and during the war for a Russian news agency and then at the Polish Embassy in London. She died in London in 2003 at the age of 93. In 1945 Kathleen married a Somalian, Sulaban Wrsama, in Stepney. She became a foster mother and died in London in 1996 at the age of 91.

Notes

1. Jonathan Croall, *Gielgud: A Theatrical Life* (Methuen, 2001), p. 18.
2. Stephen Bourne, interview with Esther Bruce, London, 1989. See also Stephen Bourne, 'My Inspirational Aunt Esther', *Guardian*, 9 July 2011 and Stephen Bourne and Esther Bruce, *Esther Bruce: A Black London Seamstress: Her Story 1912–1994* (History & Social Action Publications, 2012).
3. Bourne and Bruce, 1989.
4. Ibid.
5. Ibid.
6. Stephen Bourne, interview with Josephine Florent, London, 21 August 1995.
7. Ibid.
8. Ibid.
9. Thanks to the Black Cultural Archives for bringing the story of Kathleen Wrsama to my attention. Catalogue reference: BCA/5/1/24.

13

MABEL MERCER

When Mabel Mercer returned to London in 1977 for the first time in almost forty years to perform in cabaret at Mayfair's Playboy Club, the 77-year-old singer received ecstatic reviews. Said Jack Tinker in the *Daily Mail* (20 July 1977):

> Frank Sinatra swears he learned everything he knows about phrasing a song from Mabel Mercer; and I for one believe him. At the age of 77 this extraordinary lady has probably forgotten more than most artists are likely to learn. And she is back in London for the first time in 40 years to prove she still has plenty to teach anyone who cares to listen. In New York she is a classy cult all on her own. Singers and aficionados flock to any clubroom she graces with her stately presence. It comes as something of a shock to learn that someone who oozes the wisdom of Manhattan should have been born in smoky Staffordshire.

Jack Tinker was not the only British journalist who was surprised that the New Yorker Mabel, who had taken American citizenship in 1952, had been born in England in the final year of Queen Victoria's reign.

As an adopted American, Mabel may have been one of the most influential singers of the twentieth century, and a recipient of America's Presidential Medal of Freedom, but she was indeed born in 'smoky' Staffordshire – Burton-upon Trent, to be precise – on 3 February 1900. She was the illegitimate daughter of Emily Wadham, who described herself on the birth certificate as 'Musical Artiste'. However, the identity of her father has remained shrouded in mystery. His name does not appear on Mabel's birth certificate, but it has been claimed that he was an African American musician. His surname may have been Mercer, but this has not been verified either. Music historian Howard Rye says that the identity of Mabel's father is not securely known: 'She believed her father was Benjamin "Ben" Mercer who travelled to Britain as a merchant seaman in late 1898 and became a member of a tumbling act called The Jiminy Crickets. This is not verifiable.'[1]

Emily was the daughter of Benjamin Braffet Wadham. Deaf and dumb from childhood, he described himself as a photographer but he also has entries in several reference books on Victorian painters. Mabel described her family as 'bohemian' because they were mostly employed as painters or music hall entertainers. Mabel never lived in Staffordshire; she was raised by her grandmother in North Wales. She later said that her earliest recollections was living with her grandmother, and appreciating the countryside of North Wales, but this ended when she was sent away to be educated (1907–14) at a Catholic convent boarding school in Blackley Park, Manchester. According to her biographer, James Haskins, her family never explained to her the circumstances of her birth and parentage: 'although apparently they had prepared the nuns, who were ready with answers when she had questions [...] Her earliest inkling that she was different was that her hair was not like that of other girls.'[2] Mabel later recalled:

> At school all the kids thought I was rather odd. They'd never seen anything like me. I was the only one, you see. They christened me Golliwog, which was an affectionate term, because the 'golliwogs' the children had were little black dolls, with black woollen hair. I was always envious of the girls with long hair. The one who sat next to me in the refectory at the convent – Queenie Bale – had long flaxen hair ... I never had any more than I've got now, and it was the bane of my existence. I used to get string and braid it and tie it to my hair with a big bow so that I could flick my plaits back. I remember one little girl said to me, 'Oh, *you*'ll never get married'. And I said, 'Why?' 'Your hair's too frizzy,' she answered. 'No man will ever marry you.' And another kid said, 'We'll turn you upside down and sweep the floor with you.' And I got terribly upset because I had golliwog hair.[3]

When her beloved grandmother died in 1909, Mabel was a young pupil at the convent school. Three years later her mother, who had always been an absent figure, completely disappeared from her life when she emigrated to America in 1912 with Mabel's step-father. Mother and daughter didn't meet again for twenty-five years. This meant that, when she left school at the age of 14, in 1914, she had to support herself. At that time in Britain, young black and mixed-race girls really only had two career choices: they either went on the stage or took a job as a seamstress. In fact, this had been the case since black women began to settle in Britain in the 1600s. Work and educational opportunities for them were extremely limited, including those who came from middle-class backgrounds and had had private schooling. There were occasional job opportunities as a child's nurse (in this context, a carer or 'nanny') or in domestic service. For example, Mary Crawshaw, known as 'Giggee', born in Kingston, Jamaica, was the child's nurse who took care of Tabitha Ransome, daughter of the writer Arthur Ransome, famous for his children's book *Swallows and Amazons*. According to the 1911 census, 27-year-old Mary is a servant (entered as nurse, domestic) in the home of Tabitha's grandparents in Bournemouth.[4]

Dinah Beccles's story was also typical of young black women who were born in the colonies and brought to Britain. Born Dinah Ada Beccles in British Guiana in 1891, she was an orphan who was 'adopted' by a white British colonial family. In 1901 she travelled from Demerara in British Guiana to Southampton by ship with Mrs Catharine Stephens and her 11-year-old daughter. In 1904 Mrs Stephens was listed as Dinah's 'parent/guardian' and living at 40 Netherwood Road, Hammersmith when the child was admitted to the nearby Addison Gardens School. It has been confirmed that Dinah had been taken from an orphanage in British Guiana to assist with the upbringing of Mrs Stephens's daughter. While still only a child herself, Dinah was employed as a children's nurse.[5] However, for reasons which have not come to light, her life took a turn for the worse. In the 1911 census she is listed as a 20-year-old 'inmate' of the Convent and Home of The Good Shepherd in East End Road, East Finchley. It is described as a 'refuge for distressed Roman Catholic women'. Thereafter, and throughout the First World War and into the 1920s, Dinah worked 'in service' as a domestic servant, and this is the profession she entered on her marriage certificate when she married, in 1923, to a 49-year-old white British handyman, James Timbs.

Mabel Mercer may have avoided the exploitation of the world of domestic service, but she was not a natural for a life on the stage, either, as she later explained:

> I was *the* most self-conscious child. I don't know how I ever became an entertainer. It was absolute agony at school when I was called on to recite a poem or something. I would turn scarlet, my knees would knock, and my lips would tremble so that I could hardly pronounce the words. And there I was, the child of performers, and I couldn't get over it. Horrible, horrible. Even now when I'm going to sing a new song or appear in a new place, I get stomach-ache.[6]

After leaving school, Mabel joined her mother's older sister, her aunt Lavinia du Rocher, in a family music hall act that included Lavinia's French husband, Eugene. Consequently Mabel began her show business career just as the First World War started. In 1976 she told her friend Alec Wilder:

> I worked with part of my family in an act, my three cousins and my aunt. We'd sing songs like 'Down by the Old Mill stream' and 'Sweet and Low', things like that, in harmony. We had a good act and were popular and very successful on any bill. These were the experiences where I learned my trade. We'd travel from one country to another and I remember we found ourselves in Holland working suddenly with a circus, between the elephant acts![7]

Mabel was on stage in the family act until her cousins were called up to serve in the war. 'The act split up and I had to go out on my own.'[8] According to James Haskins, it had been a hard life:

> In Mabel's recollection, her family's troupe never made it to the coveted position of closing act [...] The bad memories she did not care to mention, but the life of a second-rate vaudeville team was also fraught with cold-hearted managers and drafty houses and the constantly looming fear of being stranded a hundred miles from home.[9]

After the act broke up, Mabel thought she knew how to sing and dance well enough to get by:

So I joined a troupe of girl dancers. When we played in Manchester, which was the home of the Tiller Girls, I asked for an audition, and they said I could go into one of their smaller troupes. So I joined the Tiller Girls – that is, until the head man saw me and said, 'Oh, out with *her*, she's not right in the line.' I was so different, you see, with my woolly head.[10]

Mabel's life changed forever when, in the middle of the First World War, she joined Will Garland's touring revue *Coloured Society*. Garland was an African-American impresario and tenor singer who, from 1904, had been producing many touring revues in England with all-black casts.[11] Throughout 1916 and 1917 his *Coloured Society* revue toured all over the country. When she joined the cast of this revue in 1916, Mabel met other black and mixed-race people for the first time. Some of them were American, but others were African, or from various British seaports, including London's East End, Cardiff and Liverpool:

Now, *that* was a first experience. I had never known any coloured people, never *met* any. Isn't that funny? My family never discussed anything, and I was the only one at school, so I just took it for granted that I was one of a kind. And finding these others was like a dream. I was delighted. We were all different shades but all the same.[12]

Mabel recalled that, for *Coloured Society*, Garland had:

Collected a few Africans and a lot of artists of mixed blood in England and put together a fine show. It was called *Coloured Society*, a very good singing and dancing show, with comedians, a regular revue. The boss [Garland] was an excellent lyric tenor, we had a big fellow from Africa with a gorgeous bass, and there were a lot of fine voices in the group. The first scene was set in Dahomey, and we were all Zulus, running around and saying 'Woo, woo, woo'. Then we'd each do our different things, and we'd wind up, believe it or not, singing the sextet from Donizetti's Italian opera *Lucia di Lammermoor*. I sang the soprano part. It was so unexpected – all those Zulus singing *Lucia*. I loved it. I never realized the incongruity of it until I was grown and wondered what *must* people have thought![13]

Though Mabel never became a star of the music halls, in addition to Will Garland and the casts of his 'all-black' shows, there were quite a number of black music hall entertainers in Britain who were popular.

Many of them, including the song and dance double act Smith and Johnson, were African-Americans who had settled in this country before 1914.[14] During the reign of Queen Victoria (1837–1901) the main contact white Britons had with black people was either in sport, mostly boxing, or in popular entertainment, such as the music halls. This continued to be the case throughout the Edwardian era and the First World War when troops who were home on leave, as well as the British public, could see a variety of black stars in music halls up and down the country. Perhaps the most famous were Scott and Whaley, a cross-talking double act. Eddie Whaley was the straight man, intelligent and smartly dressed, and Harry Scott the comedy half, appearing in blackface as the lugubrious country bumpkin. They arrived in Britain in 1909 with bookings for only eight weeks but they were so successful they never returned to the United States and became British subjects. They were among the most highly paid music hall acts of their day.[15]

There was also the glamorous singer and dancer Belle Davis, another American expatriate, who also enjoyed popularity in British music halls after her arrival here in 1901. Jeffrey Green and Rainer E. Lotz have commented:

> Her performance style changed from 'coon shouting' and 'ragtime sing-ing' in the 1890s to a more decorous manner, where prancing children provided the amusement. She directed their stage act, and with two, sometimes three or four, black children the act was a vigorous and popu-lar entertainment in British and continental theatres [...] The act had been seen by hundreds of thousands of Britons by 1914, when war prevented continental touring and so exposed more Britons to Belle Davies [*sic*] and Her Cracker Jacks. She and the children performed in major cities as well as Ayr, Doncaster, Portsmouth, Ilkeston, and Weymouth during the war years. Her last known performance in Britain was in 1918.[16]

Louis Douglas was one of the young American dancers employed by Belle Davis for her act. He toured Europe with her from 1903 to 1908 and remained in Europe afterwards. During the war Douglas enjoyed success as an 'eccentric' dancer in popular revues like *Pick-A-Dilly* (London Pavilion, 1916). During the war, The Versatile Four (some-times known as The Versatile Three), a talented quartet of vocalists, instrumentalists and dancers, worked in Britain. They were African-Americans who, in 1913, started a long residency at Murray's Club,

London which marked the beginning of the vogue for jazz in Britain. The Jamaican-born pianist Dan Kildare was also a pioneer of ragtime and jazz. He toured widely in 1915–17 and, according to the jazz historian Howard Rye, his 1917 tour with his Seven Spades was 'especially influential in exposing African-American musical developments to a wider audience'.[17]

Mabel Mercer stayed with Will Garland's *Coloured Society* and his follow-up revue *All-Black* (1917–18) until the end of the war, through the Zeppelin raids and the flu epidemic:

> That was terrible. Our conductor had such a bad case of it that he couldn't work, and my boss sent me on in his place, as a pianist/conductor down in the pit. I'd rush up on stage for my title part in *Lucia*. The conductor never rejoined us, and I continued as pianist/conductor as we travelled about, until we got to London and were to play in a large theatre with an orchestra of fifteen or sixteen men. Here I wasn't to sit at the piano, but stand and conduct, and when we went to the first rehearsal, I was scared to death. One of the greybeards in the orchestra looked at me and said, 'What can *she* do?' and my boss spoke up very strong, 'She can do exactly what I want her to do.' He took me to a boys' tailor, and they rigged me up in a silk-bosom shirt and white tie and tails, and I thought I was *IT!*[18]

Sometime during the First World War Mabel befriended Nanette Horton Boucher and her family. Nanette was the daughter of James Africanus Horton (1835–83), an African surgeon, soldier and nationalist. After marrying William Henry Boucher, Nanette had three mixed-race children: Madeleine, known as 'Dickie', in Sierra Leone in 1900; Percy, known as James, in London in 1902; and Nanette, known as Ena, in London in 1906. Jeffrey Green acknowledges in *Black Edwardians* that Nanette assisted Mabel in moving from 'risky theatrical lodgings' and that Ena and Madeleine became lifelong friends of Mabel. All three eventually settled in America.[19]

Mabel worked in Britain right up to the end of the First World War and, in the 1920s, when she based herself in Paris, she began her long and eventful career as a cabaret singer. She was perhaps the greatest cabaret artiste of her generation and, after relocating to New York in 1941, she influenced some of the great American singers of the twentieth century. Frank Sinatra, Billie Holiday, Judy Garland and Barbara

Cook were among them. She died in 1984. Said the American critic Rex Reed: 'No singer with any class has failed to be influenced by her way with a lyric or her weaving of a melody. Her achievement is a legend. I think she is the eighth wonder of the world.'[20] Says Keith Howes, who saw her in London in 1977:

Sitting straight backed in a chair, resembling a dignitary upon a throne, she held the whole room spellbound. No glitter, no glamour, just the words and the music. How would I rate her? On just this one occasion, with and possibly above Lena Horne, Ella Fitzgerald, Cleo Laine, and certainly above Diana Ross and Tina Turner, all of whom I have seen live. Her articulation! Her timing! Her gravitas mixed with a teasing sense of fun. She was ageless, magnetic. No wonder Sinatra saw her as a mentor.[21]

Notes

1. Thanks to Howard Rye for this information. See also Howard Rye, 'Mabel Mercer (1900–1984), cabaret singer', *Oxford Dictionary of National Biography* (Oxford University Press, 2004).
2. James Haskins, *Mabel Mercer: A Life* (Atheneum, 1987), p. 7.
3. William Livingstone, 'Mabel Mercer', *Stereo Review*, February 1975, p. 61.
4. Jeffrey Green, *Black Edwardians: Black People in Britain 1901–1914* (Frank Cass, 1998), p. 65.
5. Stephen Bourne, interviews with Esther Bruce, London, 1989 and Brenda Clough, London, 2013.
6. Livingstone, p. 61.
7. Alec Wilder, interview with Mabel Mercer, 'Echoes of My Life' album sleeve notes, 1976.
8. Livingstone, p. 62.
9. Haskins, p. 12.
10. Livingstone, p. 62.
11. Jeffrey Green and Rainer E. Lotz, 'Will Garland (1878–1938), theatrical entertainer', *Oxford Dictionary of National Biography* (Oxford University Press, 2004). See also Rainer E. Lotz, *Black People: Entertainers of African Descent in Europe, and Germany* (Birgit Lotz Verlag, 1997).
12. Livingstone, p. 62.
13. Ibid.
14. Stephen Bourne, 'Connie Smith (1875–1970), music-hall entertainer and actress', *Oxford Dictionary of National Biography* (Oxford University Press, 2010).
15. Stephen Bourne, 'Edward (Eddie) Whaley (*c.*1880–1961), comedian and singer', *Oxford Dictionary of National Biography* (Oxford University Press, September 2013).
16. Jeffrey Green and Rainer E. Lotz, 'Belle Davis (1874–in or after 1938), dancer and singer', *Oxford Dictionary of National Biography* (Oxford University Press, September 2004).

17. Howard Rye, 'Jazz', David Dabydeen, John Gilmore and Cecily Jones, editors, *The Oxford Companion to Black British History* (Oxford University Press, 2007), pp. 234–35 and 'Dan Kildare', *Jazz Journal*, vol. 66, no. 3, March 2013, pp. 17–19.
18. Livingstone, p. 62.
19. Green, *Black Edwardians*, p. 140.
20. Livingstone, p. 64.
21. Stephen Bourne, interview with Keith Howes, London, 7 January 2014.

14

AMANDA AND AVRIL

The daughters of two famous black men, Amanda Ira Aldridge and Avril Coleridge-Taylor, were British-born and lived in London throughout the First World War. Both of them were composers, and managed to make an impression on the conservative and male-dominated world of music.

Amanda was the daughter of Ira Aldridge (1807?–67), the celebrated African-American tragedian of the Victorian era, and his second wife, the Swedish Baroness Paulina von Brandt. Ira's acting career lasted for an awesome four decades, and most of his appearances were made in Britain and on the Continent. In 1833 he played Shakespeare's Othello at the Theatre Royal in Covent Garden. In *Ira Aldridge: The Negro Tragedian* (1958) his biographers Herbert Marshall and Mildred Stock described him as 'the first to show that a black man could scale any heights in theatrical art reached by a white man – and recreate with equal artistry the greatest characters in world drama'. He was granted British citizenship in 1863, and his name has been inscribed with other Shakespearean actors at the Shakespeare Memorial Theatre in Stratford-upon-Avon. Oku Ekpenyon, a member of the Black and Asian Studies Association, successfully campaigned for Aldridge to be honoured at London's Old Vic Theatre. The unveiling of a print of Aldridge as Aaron in Shakespeare's *Titus Andronicus* (donated by the National Portrait Gallery) took place on 24 September 2004.[1]

Ira's youngest child, Amanda, was born in 1866 at the family home, Luranah Villa, in Penge, south-east London. She was only 17 months old when her father died on tour in Lodz, Poland on 7 August 1867. He left Paulina a widow with three young children: Luranah, 7, Ira Frederick, 5, and little Amanda. The Aldridge children showed great musical promise from childhood and their mother encouraged them to have a sense of pride in their African heritage. In honour of her father, Amanda added the name Ira to her own. As a singer, one of Amanda's earliest concerts took place in Crystal Palace in 1881. She sang Handel's 'Creations Hymn' and a ballad. Two years later, at the age of 17, she won a foundation scholarship to the newly opened Royal College of Music where she studied singing with Jenny Lind, a famous opera singer who was known as the Swedish Nightingale. For many years Amanda enjoyed popularity as a contralto, often appearing with her brother as her accompanist until his early death in 1886 at the age of 25. Sadly, Amanda's singing career ended after an attack of laryngitis damaged her throat, but she remembered what Jenny Lind had said to her: 'Never mind what happens to your throat. You can always earn a livelihood as a singing teacher, because you have a good insight into voice theory and practice.'

After her singing career had ended, Amanda turned her attention to composing and teaching voice production and piano. She started composing when she was in her 30s and always published under the name Montague Ring, to separate her work as a composer from that of singing and voice teacher. She composed love songs, suites, sambas, and light orchestral pieces. Says Sophie Fuller in *The Pandora Guide to Women Composers* (1994):

> Most of her music is in a popular style, often using syncopated dance rhythms. Her best-known work is *Three African Dances* (1913) [...] The slow, central movement, 'Luleta's Dance', uses themes reminiscent of music from West Africa [...] Aldridge also published over 25 songs [and] wrote her own words for many of her earliest songs.[2]

During the First World War, Amanda resided at 2 Bedford Gardens in the London borough of Kensington and Chelsea. She never married, claiming to be too busy because, in addition to her teaching work and composition, she had to care for her elderly mother and her sister Luranah. Her mother, Paulina, died aged 81 in 1915, and Luranah, whose own successful musical career was cut short when she developed severe rheumatism, spent the last twenty years of her life as an invalid before committing suicide in 1932.

After the war, Amanda's distinguished pupils included three internationally acclaimed African-American concert singers who studied with her in London in the 1920s: Roland Hayes, Paul Robeson and Marian Anderson. The tenor Roland Hayes included many of Amanda's songs in his repertoire and, in a letter he wrote to her from America in 1919, he said: 'I find your songs so very beautiful.' Another of Amanda's students, the actor Earl Cameron, later described her as 'light skinned, rather short and stocky. She was a lively, well spoken, delicate and distinguished lady with a tremendous sense of humour. She could laugh about most things. She was a courteous, beautiful human being, but not wealthy.'[3] Amanda died the day before her 90th birthday on 9 March 1956 and was buried in an unmarked grave in Streatham Park Cemetery.[4]

Avril Coleridge-Taylor was the daughter of Samuel Coleridge-Taylor (1875–1912), one of the most celebrated composers and conductors of the Edwardian era. Samuel, born in London, was the mixed-race son of a Sierra Leonean doctor and a white British mother. In 1899 he married Jessie Walmisley and Avril had one older brother, Hiawatha, born in 1900, who was named after his father's most famous composition, *Hiawatha's Wedding Feast*. Avril was born in 1903 in South Norwood, Croydon (south London).

Avril and her brother were raised in the family home in Croydon, and mostly these were happy times, but occasionally there were ugly incidents. For example, when Avril was interviewed by the mezzo-soprano and broadcaster Carole Rosen in 1987, she recalled the trouble caused by some local school boys:

> Directly they saw father coming in the distance with my brother on one side and myself on the other, father put his hand in mine and clenched it. He knew what was going to happen. So as we came nearer to these schoolboys we knew they were going to shout all kinds of horrible things, which they did. And unfortunately on one occasion they went for my brother and fought him and the poor boy fell to the ground and was very badly hurt.[5]

Avril was only 9 years old on 1 September 1912 when her father died of pneumonia, but he had been a great influence on the young child. When Avril was interviewed by Carole Rosen, she remembered the happy times she shared with him:

We were very close. I used to go into his room where he played the piano, writing music, and I sat at his feet, near the piano, so I really absorbed everything that he wrote. And also, when we were out walking together, he used to speak about music to me, and tell me to listen to the birds singing. There was one special bird that he loved and that was the lark. All around us were cornfields and poppies growing. That was a walk he loved to take every day. He loved the country and everything that was beautiful. So that was a happy memory of mine. He was very sincere in everything and he loved children. He loved to play with them, sing to them and play the piano to them. That's why I stayed close to him, always when he was composing at the piano. I was at his feet, leaning against the piano leg, taking in all the music that I heard.[6]

As a child Avril sang and attended ballet classes but it did not take her long to commence her career in music composition when she wrote and published *Goodbye Butterfly* at the age of 12. In that same year she won a three-year Scholarship for Composition and Pianoforte to the Trinity College of Music. She studied the violin, orchestration, composition and conducting and later reflected:

Quite early in life I began to feel a sense of music within me that was anxious to make its way out. Not only did I want to write music – as I had seen my father do – but to express myself through beautiful sound. So, before I was twelve, when most other children amused themselves by playing games, I was concentrating on composition. I also taught myself to play the piano sufficiently to master difficult pieces by Beethoven and Schumann, as well as several of my father's compositions. Reading music came as naturally to me as reading books which, from the age of five, I did quite easily.[7]

During the First World War, Hiawatha volunteered for the French Red Cross and was employed by them as an ambulance driver. Avril recalled the terrifying Zeppelin raids over London that interrupted her music studies. She also took part in 'a great many wartime concerts in London, playing the piano, reciting, and appearing in sketches'.[8] Towards the end of the war, Avril made her first appearance at the Aeolian Hall, a concert hall in London's New Bond Street, at the age of 15 'reciting the story by Hans Andersen for which my father had written the music that later became the *Petite Suite*'.[9] During the war Avril travelled throughout the country singing her father's music, his songs and *Hiawatha*, which she enjoyed. 'I think that would have pleased him,' she said, 'because I knew how he wanted it to be done.'[10] Avril began writing compositions during the First World War and continued into the 1970s. In all, Avril wrote more than ninety compositions and also worked as a conductor, rare for a woman of her time. In fact, Avril was one of the few women to break down barriers in the conservative world of classical musical. Avril died in 1998 at the age of 95.[11]

Notes

1. See Heidi J. Holder, 'Ira Aldridge (1807?–1867), actor', *Oxford Dictionary of National Biography* (Oxford University Press, 2004) and Stephen Bourne, *Speak of me as I am: The Black Presence in Southwark Since 1600* (Southwark Council, 2005).
2. Sophie Fuller, *The Pandora Guide to Women Composers* (Pandora, 1994), pp. 36–37.
3. Stephen Bourne, interview with Earl Cameron, London, 4 April 1997.
4. Stephen Bourne, 'Amanda Aldridge [*pseud.* Montague Ring] (1866–1956), singer and composer', *Oxford Dictionary of National Biography* (Oxford University Press, 2004).
5. Avril Coleridge-Taylor, interview with Carole Rosen, March 1987. BBC Sound Archive.
6. Ibid.
7. Avril Coleridge-Taylor, *The Heritage of Samuel Coleridge-Taylor* (Dennis Dobson, 1979), p. 103.
8. Ibid., p. 106.
9. Ibid.
10. Rosen interview.
11. Stephen Bourne, 'Avril Coleridge-Taylor (1903–1998), composer and conductor', *Oxford Dictionary of National Biography* (Oxford University Press, 2010).

PART III:

THE 1919 RACE RIOTS

15

ERNEST MARKE: 'WE WERE JUST A SCAPEGOAT'

1919 was the first year of peace, but it was also the year in which racial tensions exploded throughout Britain. Race riots were caused by a strong feeling of unrest, fuelled by white ex-servicemen who felt that they had returned home from the battlefields to a country that was not fit for heroes. A scapegoat was needed, and in 1919 it was Britain's African and Caribbean community that was targeted, as well as citizens from Arabia and Asia. They were mostly attacked in the main British seaports where some of them had settled, but isolated attacks soon became widespread and there were extremely violent riots in seven major towns and cities between January and August 1919: Barry, Glasgow, Liverpool, London's East End, and South Shields. The most violent outbreaks took place in South Wales (Newport and Cardiff).

Ernest Marke was just a 16-year-old ex-merchant seaman when he found himself caught up in the Liverpool riots of 1919. Ernest's accounts of his terrifying ordeals at the hands of white mobs offer a first-hand insight into what it must have been like for a black citizen at that time. In 1975 Ernest wrote about the riots in his autobiography *Old Man Trouble* and when he was in his 90s he found himself in demand for interviews. In 1994 he talked about his experiences of Liverpool in 1919 in Steve Humphries's *Riots* documentary in the BBC series *Forbidden Britain: Our Secret Past 1900–1960* and also in the book that accompanied the series.

Ernest was born in Freetown, Sierra Leone, in August 1902, the son of a Sierra Leonean merchant. He was just 14 years old when he ran away from home and stowed away on the SS *Adansi*, a merchant ship bound for Liverpool. In April 1917 in the Bay of Biscay the ship was torpedoed and sunk by a German submarine. Ernest later recalled:

> The second steward and I were singing: *We haven't seen the Kaiser for a hell of a while* [...] Suddenly there was a terrific bang and the ship shuddered. We heard the ship's whistle blow the signal for all hands to muster the lifeboats. A torpedo had scored a direct hit on the port bow. The ship was going down fast.[1]

However, young Ernest survived the ordeal and found himself in the chief officer's lifeboat: 'our ship had disappeared completely and we were left on our own [...] Not a ship in sight. When the first ration of biscuit and water was distributed we found that the leading stoker was dead. There was no place for an inquest. He was dumped overboard.'[2]

After several days at sea, a British ship rescued Ernest and his shipmates: 'I couldn't climb the ladder as quickly as I had thought. Both my legs were partly paralysed and my feet were terribly swollen; but with kind helping hands I was soon aboard in a nice warm room, a warm blanket round me and a hot cup of tea.'[3]

In Liverpool Ernest lodged with the chief steward and his family in Wavertree, and attended the nearest Roman Catholic church:

> One evening while serving at the altar, there was a slight commotion in the pews. A woman had fainted and she was being taken outside for some air. When she recovered she told the people around her that she had seen a devil at the altar – me. There were very few negroes in England in those days and there were certainly none at Wavertree [...] I imagine I was the first black man she had ever seen.[4]

After joining another ship, the *Gabon*, as a cabin boy, Ernest found himself in trouble again. Another German submarine attacked his ship:

> I woke up to hear foot-steps running all over the deck, then a loud explosion like the sound of a big gun. I rushed out and ran towards the after deck [...] Then I saw that it was our gun which was in action. Some of

the crew were passing ammunition to the gunners. Shells were falling all around us. Strangely enough I wasn't at all afraid.[5]

The *Gabon* sunk the submarine: 'I have never forgotten the awesome sight of nothing but the circle of oil where the submarine had been.'[6]

At 15 Ernest decided to join the British Army. Lying about his age (he told the recruiting officer he was 18) he enlisted in a Shropshire regiment with his pal, Tommy McCauley, a young West African who was also from Sierra Leone:

That was the finest thing that ever happened to me, for apart from the military uniform, which appealed to me, it made me feel grown up. The two months I spent in the army were very happy times. I encountered no colour prejudice of any kind and the feeling that we were all in the same uniform was a strong one [...] But then the old Kaiser must have seen me coming for he decided to surrender.[7]

After being demobilised Ernest returned to Liverpool:

I found it very difficult to get a job, in fact all black people found it difficult to get work as the soldiers were coming back home from the war, and they were given preference. Where the black man had a job he was sacked so that the white man could get that job. Blacks could not get jobs even to sweep the streets. This situation of unemployment and the racist reaction by the whites to the black man was the main reason behind the race riots of 1919 in Liverpool, Cardiff, and even Glasgow. Because of this, black people were offered free passages (repatriation) to Africa or the West Indies. The Government offered £6 for each black person taking up the offer. £1 to be given on embarkation, and £5 on arrival at the destination.[8]

Recalling the Liverpool riots of 1919 for BBC television's *Forbidden Britain* in 1994, Ernest said:

I was in civvies and I went around the corner [...] Suddenly a crowd says, 'Here's one of them niggers, get him.' Oh my God, I started running and good job I wasn't far off where my house was but before I could get there some women with clogs on and shawls over their heads says to this mob, 'Leave him alone, he hasn't done anything to you'. So I got away. On another occasion myself and this boy from St Lucia we got off the bus at Lime Street, walking towards the Adelphi Hotel, when suddenly this crowd saw us, like a pack of wolves they started chasing us. They was shouting 'black bastard, nigger.' We really were frightened. Again it was a woman who saved me. She heard the noise and opened her window telling us to go round the corner and through the back alley, she opened the back gate for us and in we went. The crowd passed, they couldn't find us. I really thought we were gonna be killed that time and I had actually knew this bloke who was killed with the riot you see, killed by one of these crowds.[9]

It was a 24-year-old Bermudian seaman called Charles Wotten who was murdered (see Chapter 18), sending shock waves throughout Liverpool's black community. Said Ernest: 'After that I bought a razor, most of the boys carried razors, not to hurt anyone but just for their own protection. And when the next mob started coming towards me they cornered me so I pulled out this razor and started slashing, they ran.'[10] Ernest said that the police refused to help black victims because some of them were very prejudiced, but he also understood some of the underlying reasons for the violence that surfaced in the white community.

Ernest blamed unemployment, partly caused by the closing down of munitions factories. Unemployment, he said, usually led to unrest and starvation and these, in turn, made people look for a scapegoat. The white mobs vented their anger and frustration on the black men who happened to be in a small minority and the 'underdog':

It wasn't really hatred of the blacks you see, it's jobs, we were just a scape-goat. They just come from the army and they forget we also come from the front line, well, that's the human race see, they're selfish [...] Sexual jealousy is there, 'I don't want my daughter going with a goddamn nigger.' The hatred just comes automatically. One or two just want violence but they're the biggest cowards of all, they'll run like mad if they're not in a mob.[11]

Ernest died in London in 1995 at the age of 93. His obituarist, Val Wilmer, described him as 'articulate and forceful, he was in constant demand to talk at conferences and gatherings of black Britons through-out the country, celebrated as a survivor and strategist who had never eaten humble pie nor bowed his knee to the white man'.[12]

Notes

1. Ernest Marke, *Old Man Trouble* (Weidenfeld and Nicholson, 1975), p. 9.
2. Ibid., p. 13.
3. Ibid.
4. Ibid., p. 14.
5. Ibid., p. 15.
6. Ibid., p. 16.
7. Ibid., p. 25.
8. Don Henry, *Thirty Blacks in British Education: Hopes, Frustrations, Achievements* (Rabbit Press, 1991), p. 26.
9. Steve Humphries and Pamela Gordon, *Forbidden Britain: Our Secret Past 1900-1960* (BBC Books, 1994), pp. 103–04.
10. Ibid., p. 104.
11. Ibid.
12. Val Wilmer, *The Guardian*, 16 September 1995, p. 30. See also Stephen Bourne, 'Ernest Marke (1902–1995), seaman and club owner', *Oxford Dictionary of National Biography* (Oxford University Press, 2012).

16

LONDON'S EAST END

On 22 June 1948 the *Empire Windrush* docked at Tilbury bringing nearly 500 passengers from Jamaica in search of work. This voyage is now recognised as a key event in the history of black settlers in Britain and the start of post-war settlement from Africa and the Caribbean. However, there had been a black presence in Britain long before the 'Windrush Generation' came to these shores. Britain's ports, such as London, Cardiff and Liverpool, had been attracting black settlers for over 150 years.

Black people had been settling in London's East End as far back as the beginning of the eighteenth century. Michael Banton noted in *The Coloured Quarter* (1955) that in the early 1700s:

> Coloured men were to be found in Stepney [...] According to local tradition there were two inns by the river in Wapping which made a market for the sale of young slaves as domestic servants [...] At the same time coloured seamen were coming into the port and spreading into the nearby parishes.[1]

Banton also quoted a curate of a Stepney clergyman, Dr Mayo (1733–91), who was 'particularly kind to the negroes and uninstructed men of colour, who, employed generally on board of ship, occasionally resided in his parish, which is full of seafaring people'.[2] Towards the end of the nineteenth century a small black settlement had grown near the docks in Canning Town. Banton said:

The men were mostly West Indians and seamen [...] Some of the coloured people alive in Stepney today were born in Canning Town about this time, and they say that the white and coloured people in the neighbourhood were on very good terms and there was little colour consciousness, but that relations deteriorated later.[3]

By the start of the First World War, a number of black families and seamen were living in the area around the Royal Group of Docks in the East End. These docks were the largest in the world, and the Port of London was the most famous in the British Empire. Merchant seamen could be found residing in lodging houses, and many black families settled in the streets around the 'sailortown' area of Victoria Dock Road which ran from west to east from Canning Town to Custom House. The number of African and West Indian seamen who settled in the area increased during the First World War. Historian Howard Bloch has researched the lives of the East End's black community between the wars:

Some black men chose to make new homes in London while others, because of the downturn in world trade, and the colour bar, found it difficult to obtain a passage home. Many of them settled in the streets around the 'sailortown' area [...] The number of black seamen who settled in the district increased during the First World War. Some black men stowed away on ships from the Caribbean in order to volunteer to fight with the British armed forces [...] Many of them served in the Merchant Navy.[4]

As Michael Banton writes:

Many seamen deserted or left their ships to take up shore work at the current high rates of pay, others worked their passage to Britain having heard of the opportunities for employment there. A number of ships with coloured crews were taken over by the government for transport purposes and their crews put ashore. Some of the coloured men seeking work were recruited into labour battalions for overseas service and later demobilized in Britain. After the war the shipping industry was forced to contract, and with the demobilization of ex-servicemen the level of unemployment rose everywhere. Trade Unions insisted upon the prior employment of Englishmen and large numbers of coloured men were unable to get work.[5]

During and after the war, many of the black men who had settled in the East End married local white women and raised families. Mixed marriages and the employment they secured caused resentment from some of the local white population. Situated off Victoria Dock Road, Crown Street was known locally as 'Draughtboard Alley' because black and white families lived side by side. A typical mixed-race family of this era were the Coziers. After the war they lived in Sandford Street in Canning Town. The head of the household, Joseph Cozier, was born in British Guiana in 1896 and ran away to sea at the age of 14. His eldest daughter, Anita, takes up the story:

> Dad always wanted to come here. He thought England was marvellous. He was just 14 when he stowed away on a ship and came all that way from British Guiana. During World War One, Dad was a chief cook in the navy, and his ship was torpedoed three times. After the war, Dad came here, to the East End, and stayed in a lodging house in Victoria Dock Road. Mrs Mackenzie took in all the coloured seamen as lodgers. Her lodging house was near Custom House Station where the park is now.[6]

In 1920 Joseph married Florence Tindling, a white British East Ender, and they had eight children. Anita recalled that there were very few black women in their community: 'So black seamen married white women and quite a lot of mixed marriages turned out all right because they were good to each other. Where we lived there was no feeling that mixed marriages were wrong. The white people we lived with accepted it.'[7] Anita's brother Christopher has described their father as:

> [A] very educated communist who could speak three languages [...] he always found work. He took menial jobs on the railways. Dad was respected in our community. Everyone called him 'Mr. Cozier'. All the old coloured men were respected and addressed as 'Mr'. White and black people respected each other. When I grew up in the 1930s, racial prejudice did not exist in our community.[8]

However, as early as July 1917 the homes of black men and their families in Crown Street were targeted and attacked by racist outsiders, white gangs who resented their presence, and the attacks began again after the end of the war.

On 16 April 1919 there was a confrontation in Cable Street, Stepney. A violent street fight took place during which shots were fired and several black seamen were injured. The following day *The Times* reported on what they described as a serious 'East-End riot'. They claimed it had arisen 'out of the feud which has existed for some time between white and coloured seamen arriving at the Port of London [...] A number of coloured seamen were injured before the police quelled the disturbance.'[9] Tension and violent confrontations continued into the following month. On the three successive nights between 27 and 29 May white mobs attacked some of the boarding houses where black seamen lived, and attacked any black person they could find. However, when black men fought back, a number of them found themselves arrested for carrying revolvers even though they could have been carrying weapons for their own self-defence. *The Times* continued to report on the attacks:

> Renewed demonstrations of angry feeling against negroes occurred in Limehouse last night, when a large body of police were employed until a late hour quelling disturbances. Large crowds assembled outside the Asiatic Home in West India Dock Road and any coloured man who appeared was greeted with abuse, and had to be escorted by the police. It was necessary at times to bar the doors of the home. In the streets where coloured men are lodging crowds assembled, and attempts at mobbing were made both against the coloured men and against the girls with whom they are supposed to have been associated.[10]

In addition to *The Times*, a local newspaper, *East End News* (30 May 1919), also reported the incidents:

> Investigation of the cause of the trouble shows that most of the coloured men are South African Negroes, but that there is a mixture of other coloured races, who have been unable to return on the outgoing boats, which are now mostly manned by white seamen. The population about the docks has increased a great deal since the war, and residents say that many young girls have taken up with coloured men, who have lavished money on them, much to the annoyance of their white men friends.[11]

In *Under the Imperial Carpet: Essays in Black History 1780–1950*, Jacqueline Jenkinson says that the disturbances of late May 1919 led to four black men being arrested. These included John Martin, a

29-year-old Jamaican on four weeks' leave from the Royal Navy. Martin was outside a seamen's hostel, the Sailors' Home, in St Anne's Street, Limehouse when he was attacked by a group of white men. Martin was found not guilty when charged with assaulting one of the white men with a revolver. Says Jenkinson:

> He had been attacked by a mob and had been injured on the head and face. Four whites were also arrested, and two more were fined two pounds and threatened by the magistrate with more severe sentences if the trouble continued. A spokesman for the police said that white roughs had started the riots by attacking coloured men, many of whom were British: if the whites had left the blacks alone, and the authorities had repatriated the unemployed black workers, there would be no trouble.[12]

On 29 May 1919 a black seaman called William Samuel, who was lodging at the Sailors' Home in St Anne's Street, wrote a passionate letter addressed to the Colonial Secretary. In the letter he complained about the attacks on black men on the streets of London's East End:

> We beg to remind you, as at least, inform you we are boycotted in this country [...] by the same people whom less than a year ago our blood was shed on the battlefields for your safety. Laying that aside we were brutally and most barbarously attacked two nights during this week without reasonable occasion. We are making this appeal to you for the safety of your people as well as ours for we do not believe in walking along the streets of civilised London and been [being] fired at like dogs without offering any resistance [...] no black man has yet proved disloyal to any country to which he has been subjected [...] all we want is to ask Great Britain to allow us to get out of here to Japan or other countries where we have friends for England is our enemy not our friend. We beg to remind you a sergeant of police said to us last night [...] we want you niggers to get out of our country, this is a white man's country and not yours. So you see sir that it is only reasonable for you to see we are not wanted here, so please make an effort to get us out of here as quick as possible.[13]

After the 1919 riots, the East End's African, Caribbean, Indian, Malay and Chinese communities found themselves with a popular leader, Pastor Kamal Chunchie (1886–1953). After the war, many black ex-servicemen settled in the East End, married and raised families.

Kamal could empathise with them because he had also served the British in the First World War. Born in Ceylon, India in 1886, he was the eldest son of a Muslim family. In the First World War he enlisted in the 24th Middlesex Regiment, seeing action in France and Salonika.[14] He was wounded twice, and while convalescing in Malta in 1917 he converted to Christianity. After suffering from chronic malaria due to climate conditions, Kamal was discharged from the Royal Army Service Corps on 1 August 1919. His commanding officer described him as a 'well educated man and a linguist' and it was his fluency in four languages that helped him to secure a job in London's East End. However, following his arrival in the area, Kamal was faced with an appalling act of racism, as he later recalled:

> I met an English sailor lad, down and out. I took him to a magnificent building. I saw outside this building in large letters 'All Seamen Welcome'. It was a beautiful place, scrupulously clean. I asked the lad to sit at one of the tables, went over to the counter, placed a shilling and asked the English girl for two cups of tea and a piece of cake. The girl stared at me and said 'We don't serve niggers here!' What hurt the most was, behind that girl, on the wall, I read in large letters, 'God is Love'. I left the place and gave the lad the shilling.[15]

In 1920 Kamal married Mabel Tappan, a former member of the Women's Army Auxiliary Corps and in the following year he was appointed to the Queen Victoria Seaman's Rest. He was given responsibility for work among black and Asian sailors. Kamal visited the ships moored in the Thames and the Docks, as well as lodging houses and slums; he also visited the sick in hospitals in Canning Town and Greenwich. Kamal was especially concerned to relieve the poverty of poor people and did much to help with their welfare, collecting food and clothing parcels and money for medicine.

Kamal set up the Coloured Men's Wesleyan Methodist Church in a rented hall in Canning Town. This was used for social events and for Sunday school work. The work grew from fifty to about 200 black and Asian people. Later, Kamal received approval and secured funds to purchase a former lodging house. The building was located in 13–15 Tidal Basin Road, E16, and opened in 1926. The Coloured Men's Institute became a popular centre for social, welfare and religious activities with Kamal as its first pastor and warden.[16]

Among the many mixed-race couples who were living in the East End at the time of the 1919 race riots were the Elvys. On 23 February 1919 Charles Elvy, a Jamaican seaman, married the white British East Ender, Florence Humphreys, at St Luke's Church in the Victoria Docks area. At that time they were living at nearby 19 Pacific Road. Their grand-daughter, Linda Lewis, recalls:

My grandfather was a merchant seaman, a stoker, and he had fought in World War One. We were told that his ship was torpedoed. When the boats were docked, my grandmother, who was a cockney, worked on them as a cleaner. That's probably how she met my grandfather. They were married and had a family, including my mother who was born in 1929. Florence was tough as old boots and if anyone said anything offen-sive about her children or grandchildren, she would fight back. So there was prejudice and the 1919 race riots created a lot of tension between black and white people. This was still the case after the *Second* World War because I remember my mother's step-father John, who I called grand-dad, never left the house without looking smart, and carrying a gun or a knife in his back pocket, just in case he faced any trouble. The older gen-eration of West Indians did that.[7]

In spite of the prejudice they faced, Linda says that in the old days all the black and mixed-race families lived close together and looked out for each other: 'That's how Crown Street came to be named "Draughtboard Alley". The families lived in two-up, two-down houses and everyone had their doors open.'[8]

Notes

1. Michael Banton, *The Coloured Quarter: Negro Immigrants in an English City* (Jonathan Cape, 1955), pp. 22–23.
2. Ibid., p. 23.
3. Ibid., p. 27.
4. Howard Bloch, 'Black People in Canning Town and Custom House between the Wars', *Association for the Study of African, Caribbean and Asian Culture and History in Britain*, Newsletter 14 (January 1996), p. 5.
5. Banton, p. 33.
6. Stephen Bourne, interview with Anita Bowes, London, 27 January 1996.
7. Ibid.
8. Stephen Bourne, interview with Christopher Cozier, London, 1 March 1996.
9. 'East-End Riot', *The Times*, 17 April 1919, no. 42077, p. 7.
10. 'Negroes in the East-End', *The Times*, 30 May 1919, no. 42133, p. 9.

11. *East End News*, 30 May 1919, p. 5.
12. Jacqueline Jenkinson, 'The 1919 Race Riots in Britain: A Survey', Rainer Lotz and Ian Pegg, editors, *Under the Imperial Carpet: Essays in Black History 1780–1950* (Rabbit Press, 1986), p. 192.
13. William Samuel to Colonial Secretary, 29 May 1919, PRO CO 318/352.
14. When he joined the 24th Middlesex Regiment in Northampton on 19 March 1916, Kamal Chunchie spelled his christian name Kamall in his army enlistment papers, and gave his pre-war profession as a police inspector in Ceylon.
15. Geoffrey Bell, *The Other EastEnders: Kamal Chunchie and West Ham's Early Black Community* (Eastside Community Heritage, 2002), p. 2.
16. For further information see Rozina Visram, 'Kamal Athon Chunchie (1886–1953), Methodist minister and race relations worker', *Oxford Dictionary of National Biography* (Oxford University Press, 2004) and The Newham Story www. newhamstory.com
17. Stephen Bourne, interview with Linda Lewis, London, 7 September 2013.
18. Ibid.

17

BUTETOWN, CARDIFF

There is a legend that claims it was a Portuguese seaman in the early
nineteenth century who gave the name Tiger Bay to Butetown, a tiny
area situated in the Cardiff docklands of South Wales. Violent storms
made the seaman's voyage up the estuary so terrible that he said it was
like entering a bay of tigers.' After the regeneration of Tiger Bay in the
1960s, when the area was demolished to make way for a new housing project, it was renamed Cardiff Bay or The Bay, but for the locals
who took pride in their culturally diverse community, it would always
be known as Tiger Bay. During the nineteenth century South Wales
was at the centre of the European industrial revolution with Cardiff
exporting coal, iron and steel from the Welsh valleys. All the main sea
routes of Europe connected with Butetown and many of the seamen
who were working on British ships were black labourers from the colonies. Butetown became home to a mixture of nationalities towards the
end of the nineteenth century when Queen Victoria was still ruling the
British Empire. Some of these were African and West Indian seaman
who married white Welsh or English women and raised families.

Until the 1960s the popular image of Tiger Bay was an exotic but
immoral hotbed of prostitution, gambling and violence, but this stere-
otypical and racist view perpetuated by Britain's tabloid newspapers
was always refuted by the people who lived there. What the newspapers chose to ignore was the feeling of solidarity that existed in one
of Britain's most culturally diverse communities. In Colin Prescod's

documentary *Tiger Bay is My Home* (1983), the St Lucian seaman Kenneth Trotman said:

> You never miss your island when you're down in Butetown because everybody lived like one big family. Don't matter what colour you was or where you were from. Everybody was one. I never was hungry once in Cardiff because there was always somebody with a cup of tea, or a parcel of chips. People used to live as one. No selfish people was around then.[2]

When the anthropologist Kenneth Little made a study of Cardiff's black community for his book *Negroes in Britain* (1948) he described the oldest inhabitant as a Barbadian 'who made his first trip to Britain on a sailing vessel to Porthcawl, and settled in Sophia Street [Butetown] in 1885 [...] there were a few coloured men already about at this time, but their presence evoked nothing more than friendly comment.'[3] Further investigation reveals that the Barbadian was Edward Bovell who, in his latter years, remembered the race riots of 1919 and long periods of unemployment after the First World War. He had worked as a ship's cook until 1940 and then served as an air-raid warden in Tiger Bay during the Second World War. Bovell, who was believed to be Tiger Bay's oldest resident, died in St David's Hospital, Cardiff on 18 February 1961 at the age of 94.

It was in the 1890s that Butetown's black settlers started to build a community. Kenneth Little identifies Loudoun Square as the area where most Africans and West Indians lived. One of the earliest known mixed-race families in Butetown was documented in Paul Thompson's *The Edwardians* (1975). Interviewed for the book, Edith Pervoe, born in 1890, is disguised by the author as 'Harriet Vincent'. She describes her birthplace as her father's boarding house for seamen. Her father, John Joseph Pervoe, had been born in the 1850s in Nova Scotia, Canada, of West Indian parents. He gave up the sea to make a home in Butetown with his white Welsh wife, Mary Ann, towards the end of the 1880s. At the time of the 1891 census the family were living at 36 Peel Street in Butetown and John was working as a baker. He was also providing a home for several boarders who were seamen and these include three who are described as West Indian. John also had a 16-year-old servant girl living at the address, which suggests that the Pervoe family enjoyed a higher standard of living than most Butetown residents. Said Edith: 'I had all my clothes made in the dress-maker's [...] Bought everything that we wanted. Nothing second-hand.'[4] Mr Pervoe was a strict father, very religious, hated swearing, was a teetotaller and had his suits made by a Scots tailor. As Thompson said: 'There was [...] a definite attempt to insulate the children from some of the social dangers of their surroundings.'[5] The 'social dangers' were mainly street fighting caused by drunkenness. Said Edith: 'It would be the drink. They [neighbours] were quite different sober.'[6] It was the street fighting that gave Butetown its reputation for being a rough, tough neighbourhood but Mr Pervoe raised his children to respect everybody. As Edith said:

> My father tell you, 'if you give respect you can command it'. If anybody was in trouble we all helped one another. Many times I've gone round collecting for people [...] somebody died you know and perhaps they was short. I've gone out collecting for the funeral many times like that.[7]

By the time of the 1901 census John Pervoe had taken over three houses in Peel Street, and he was described as a 'seaman's lodging house keeper'. A servant was listed, as well as eight boarders, half of whom were from the West Indies. Edith told Paul Thompson:

> My father had two houses, and he had them knocked into one [...] Only the front bedrooms in the one house were let to the boarders, the others we used downstairs for ourselves [...] all seamen, seamen boarders [...] We dare not go in there. In fact he wouldn't let us in there. We weren't allowed in that part where the men were [...] My father used to do the cooking for the men [...] If my father would go to the docks with men sometimes taking their clothes to the ships, my mother would do the cooking, in the afternoons. But always my father done the most – made pastry and everything. And he had only one hand. His right hand was off, from his wrist, from an accident in a saw mill in Canada. Before he ever came to England. Do everything with it, make bread, anything. He cut the boys' hair [...] He had the power in his other hand. Only a stump. We used to call it 'Joey' when we was kids. He used to laugh a lot with us. But if he hit you with it you'd know it. Oh my God. Hard.[8]

When Edith was interviewed by William Raynor for the *Radio Times* in 1974, she recalled that her Welsh mother made her conscious – and proud – of her colour but 'you could always be in trouble if you wanted, and I was always fighting in the playground at school. I had very thick frizzy hair and when they started calling me 'nigger' and all that, I'd go for 'em first. After a while they didn't notice, and we went about as boys and girls together.'⁹ Mr Pervoe was highly respected in Butetown and he was remembered by Donald John in Jeffrey Green's *Black Edwardians* (1998) as:

> The man who always took the lead in every black funeral procession in Tiger Bay. These were quite spectacular affairs [...] Pervoe would be immaculate in black topper and a morning coat, white gloves, spats, and looking quite splendid, as he headed a retinue of similarly dressed black men walking in front of the hearse [...] sometimes the funerals were not only those of black departed, but of white people [...] perhaps the white wife of some West Indian or African, sometimes a well known white resident, but such was the respect accorded to every resident that it made no difference, Tiger Bay being such a well knit society of all its inhabitants, black or white, but always walking in front would be Mr Pervoe.¹⁰

In 1908 Edith married the Barbadian seaman James Newton Grant, one of her father's boarders. Relocating to the Rhondda valley, James worked in the pits for four years before the couple decided to return to Butetown. James then went back to sea, where he died, and in 1916 Edith married another Barbadian seaman, Charles Bryan. Her father John Pervoe died in 1943 and Edith died at the age of 89 in 1979.

Donald John, who recalled Mr Pervoe for the historian Jeffrey Green, was born James Macdonald John in 1911 at 2 Thomas Terrace, Working Street, Cardiff. His father, Elvin John, was a sailor from Barbuda who decided to raise his children away from Butetown. Elvin married Maria Thomas, a Swansea woman, and they had four sons and two daughters. The family relocated to Butetown's neighbouring, predominantly white dockland community of Grangetown because Elvin did not want his children exposed to the streetfighting and drinking atmosphere of Tiger Bay.¹¹ Elvin was working in the Cardiff docks when he died in 1924, and Donald later described to the jazz historian Val Wilmer what he found in Tiger Bay around the time of the First World War:

> I first went to Tiger Bay when my father was alive though he forbade us to ever go there. I used to sneak down with my brother Bully – we'd heard it was a wild place with lots of black people there. So one Sunday we went off and we got to Bute Road, a long road with a series of shops and cafes and almost every one was a brothel though we didn't know what a

brothel was. There'd be these girls sitting outside on chairs with their legs crossed, they'd say come here darling and they used to rub our heads for luck and give us some coppers.[12]

Donald discovered that, unlike other areas of Cardiff, in the culturally diverse community in Tiger Bay, there was no racism: 'all those black faces and nobody saying "Nigger!"'[13]

After adopting the professional name of Don Johnson, Donald became one of Cardiff's pioneering black singers. From 1937 to 1940 he was the main featured vocalist with Ken Johnson's West Indian Dance Orchestra. Another member of Ken Johnson's band was Joe Deniz, a guitarist who was born in 1913 in Butetown's Christina Street. His father, Antoni, was born in St Vincent, Cape Verde Islands, off the west coast of Africa.[14] The previously uninhabited islands were discovered and colonised by the Portuguese in the fifteenth century and became important during the Atlantic slave trade. Joe's mother, Gertrude, was Welsh of African-American and English ancestry. Joe and his older brother Frank attended South Church Street School in the bay area of Butetown; Antoni worked on the ships as a Donkeyman, keeping the ship's engines in good working order, and he would have been employed in the Merchant Navy all through the First World War. When he was away from home, Antoni would send £9 from his £18 salary to Cardiff, and as a boy Joe would be sent to collect his father's wages from the shipping line's officials. He later recalled how the Cardiff officials would make it seem as if they were being charitable when they handed over his father's hard-earned money.[15]

Butetown's reputation for criminality was refuted by Joe who told the historian Jeffrey Green that it was normal practice for neighbours to leave their front doors unlocked during the day, and that visiting each other's homes was casual. Neighbours would open the front door and announce themselves. Says Green:

The visiting foreign sailors were easy pickings for the Butetown 'entertainers' [prostitutes], but the district was not without charm. The fine old merchant houses were occupied by both blacks and whites [...] The Arabs, Somalis, Jamaicans, Africans, Malays, Chinese, Maltese and Spanish mixed with a few Egyptians and both Welsh and English. One of Joe Deniz's friends had an Italian father; another had a Norwegian father. It was 'a real community'.[16]

During the First World War the black population in Cardiff increased from 700 in 1914 to 3,000 by April 1919. As Kenneth Little writes:

During the war of 1914–18 their numbers were very greatly augmented by several streams of immigration. The war brought to Great Britain many coloured men who in normal circumstances would have been repatriated by the Government to their own country. For example, a large number of ships which ordinarily operated on the West African and other routes on which Negroes and other coloured seamen are usually employed, were requisitioned by the Government for transport service, and their crews left behind [...] this [...] influx put a final seal on the changes in character of the district and established Loudoun Square itself, with the adjoining streets, quite definitely as the coloured quarter of the city [...] Such, then, was the position at the end of the First World War. There was good money to be earned at sea during the war period and up to 1919, and the coloured men prospered.[17]

During the First World War nearly 15,000 merchant seamen were killed, with 2,500 ships sunk. Many black merchant seamen lost their lives. For example, in 1917 the troopship SS *Mendi*, carrying the final contingent of the South African Labour Corps, was sunk by the Germans off the Isle of Wight in the English Channel with the loss of 646 lives. Those who perished included 616 South Africans – 607 of them black troops – plus thirty British crew members. The loss of the SS *Mendi* was one of the worst maritime disasters of the twentieth century in British waters.[18]

In 1972 an unidentified clergyman, who was living in Cardiff during the First World War, summarised the bravery and important contribution of black seamen to the war. The 'coloured troops' he referred to were recruited from the British West Indies Regiment (see Chapter 5):

I was attached to a Labour Exchange in Cardiff. Things were bad then: submarines had turned the sea into a sailor's grave. Just then they transferred two hundred men from the coloured troops in Mesopotamia to work in the Merchant Marine. Jolly nice chaps they were: they all passed through my hands. It was a time of national crisis; and they were jolly brave those coloured sailors. They brought food to Cardiff at the greatest risk of their lives.[19]

In addition to Elvin John and his family, Butetown's neighbouring dockland community of Grangetown was also home to several other mixed-race families. During the First World War, Grangetown's Somerset Street was home to the merchant seaman James Augustus Headley who originated from Bridgetown, Barbados. He was known as 'Iron Ford' because of his temper and stern character. He married a Lancashire lass called Agnes Jolly and in 1910 their daughter Beatrice was born. At the time of Beatrice's birth, the Headley family were living in a lodging house in Peel Street, and Edith Pervoe's mother was the midwife who delivered the baby. During the war, James Headley was aboard a British ship when the Germans torpedoed it three times. His grandson, Neil Sinclair, later recalled in *The Tiger Bay Story* (1993):

> James was taken prisoner and placed in shackles aboard a German ship. It was indeed fortunate for him that this war was fought before the 'pure race' philosophy had come to power as he never complained of mistreatment by the Germans and always spoke of the German soldier who used to give him his own dinner throughout the entire ordeal. When he did finally return home he had earned two bronze medals for his bravery in service to the King. By the time the war wound down, James was home.[20]

Neighbours to the Headley family were another mixed-race couple, Nathan 'Joe' Friday and his wife Maggie. Joe came from the Caribbean island of St Vincent and had settled in the Butetown area around 1908–09. In the 1911 census Joe was listed as a seaman boarding in Butetown's Maria Street with other West Indian seaman, mostly from Jamaica. The boarding house keeper was a Jamaican called Uriah Erskine, married with a young family. By the end of the First World War, Joe had made his home in Cardiff and, with his wife Maggie, relocated to Grangetown's Somerset Street. In 1919 both the Headley family and Joe Friday were to experience first-hand the anti-black violence of the Cardiff riots.

In 1919 black and minority ethnic communities came under fire in many of the British seaports, but the worst violence occurred in south Wales. Interviewed in 1983 for Colin Prescod's documentary *Tiger Bay is My Home*, Beatrice Sinclair (formerly Headley) described Tiger Bay as 'just like a little village, about a mile, and everybody knew everyone else. We were very very happy.'[21] Beatrice said that the Cardiff riots started because white men returning from the war discovered that there was no work for them. They resented the fact that the numbers of black men in Butetown had increased during the war, and had found employment there. The fact that some of them had married local white women – and as merchant seamen had been paid much higher wages than white seamen in the Royal Navy – also contributed to their sense of frustration. Beatrice said, 'they immediately turned on us.'[22]

The tensions between the white and black communities exploded into violence in Newport on 6 June 1919. Said Alan Llwyd in *Black Wales: A History of Black Welsh People* (2005):

Many were injured [...] Newport's black citizens tried to defend themselves against their assailants with pokers and by firing pistols above their heads. The police arrested 20 black men but only two whites. 'We are all one in Newport and mean to clear these niggers out,' said one of the rioters to a *South Wales News* reporter.[23]

The anger spread into other communities of south Wales, but most of the violence occurred in Cardiff.

In Somerset Street, Grangetown, the rioters broke into the home of James Augustus Headley and his family. His daughter, Beatrice, had been celebrating her 9th birthday:

I had a birthday party and all my friends and neighbours came in [...] And that same night we had the party someone came rushing in and said 'You better hide him', pointing at my father. He said there's something going on down the street. They've attacked two houses further down and yours will be the next. So he grabbed my father and took him out the back and hid him in the lavatory. Then bang, the door went. There was pandemonium. They did hit her [Beatrice's mother] and we rushed upstairs. I said to my mother 'let's hide under the bed' because I was getting really scared.[24]

Beatrice's daughter, Leslie Clarke, has also recalled what she was told about that terrible night in her grandparents' home:

My grandparents were caught up in the riots [...] It's not a nice episode. My grandparents' home was ransacked and looted, and they had nothing left. My grandmother was badly beaten, and I believe my grandfather would have been killed if my grandmother hadn't persuaded him to escape through the back door and over the garden wall. He got away from the district altogether. My mother had to watch her mother being beaten, and when the police eventually arrived at the house, instead of commiserating with her, she was told it was her own fault for marrying a black man. This obviously made my grandfather quite a bitter person for a while. The only reason the house wasn't burned to the ground, which was what the looters wanted to do, was because it was a rented property.[25]

In a BBC television interview in 1974, 87-year-old Nathan 'Joe' Friday experienced the violence first-hand. He recalled: 'Policeman tell me "you better get out of it, mate, or you'll get into trouble." That night they come here and mash up the front window. Come to get me out. Well, I wouldn't go out. I stood there with me gun in me hand and a poker.' Unfortunately the rioters returned and smashed up and ransacked the home of Joe and his wife, in spite of the protestations of some of his white neighbours. Afterwards, Joe had to get a handcart to take the stones out of his front room. 'They broke all the glass in the front room, a wardrobe, a chest of drawers, and they take all my wife's clothes,' he said.[26]

In Butetown on 11 June 1919 the riot started after a white crowd had assaulted a group of black seamen returning from a day out with their wives. Says Neil Evans: 'Shots were fired in self defence and around the same time a white ex-soldier was found with his throat cut – allegedly, but never proved – by a black man [...] there was a (false) belief that white people had made sacrifices for the war effort while blacks had benefited.'[27] Two thousand white people attacked shops and houses associated with black citizens: 'Many were willing and even eager to participate in the negro-hunting which had developed into something like a fever,' wrote a *Western Mail* reporter.[28] The violence escalated on 12 June and a company of the Welsh Regiment had to be secretly drafted into Cardiff to help the police. Edward Scobie described the 'carefully planned assault' in *Black Britannia*:

Very early in the evening a huge crowd gathered near the Hayes Bridge, and the commotion finally settled in Millicent Street off Bute Street. White rioters stormed a house in which eight black men lived and began firing revolver shots. They were hidden in the warehouses of a wholesale grocer who lived across the street. Two soldiers in uniform led the mob. When a party of armed blacks barred the way the soldiers ordered them to drop back. They advanced again, this time holding up a table before them as a shield. Fighting began in the house with the blacks defending themselves with razor blades and a single revolver. A yelling white crowd stood outside exhorting their men and enjoying the onslaught on the besieged blacks. After a considerable time the police and fire brigade managed to intervene. The black men were taken away to the police station in what was described as 'protective custody' [...] Black men who lived in Cardiff at the time said later that during the riots they were compelled to stay in their houses behind boarded windows and barred doors.[29]

In his report to the Home Office the Chief Constable of Cardiff stated that whites were the cause of the trouble and expressed sympathy for the culturally diverse seafaring community, especially the Arabs, but nevertheless advised that unemployed 'coloured' seamen be repatriated as soon as possible.

It was a West Indian intellectual and activist called Dr Rufus E. Fennell (1887–1974) who acted as a spokesman for the community that had found itself under siege. He had trained as a doctor in the United States and, as a British subject, had served as a medic in the British Army during the First World War. He had taken care of thousands of wounded British troops in Mesopotamia and received wounds himself on at least three occasions. After the war his American medical qualifications were not recognised in Britain, so he earned a living as a dentist in Pontypridd. On 25 April 1919 he married Eilly Crane in Merthyr Tydfil, but when the riots started, Dr Fennell came to Cardiff to offer assistance and advice. During the riots Dr Fennell addressed the crowd, and a photograph of him was published in the *Western Mail* of 14 June. He is not named, but described as 'A man of colour' who advised the black community to avoid trouble: 'The doctor [...] addressed a gathering at great length, pointing out the advisability of keeping within the law and doing nothing that would excite further disorders.'

In 1978 the historian Neil Evans interviewed James Ernest, a veteran of the black community in Cardiff, about Dr Fennell. Ernest had settled in Cardiff in 1915 after arriving from St Lucia in the West Indies in a captured vessel, via a number of ports. Ernest, who continued to go to sea until the early 1950s, remembered Fennell for his 'courage and intelligence' amidst the 1919 riots. As Evans noted, 'from the disturbances' Fennell emerged as 'a dominating leader' who 'quickly assumed leadership of the coloured community [...] during the riots he was said to have walked boldly into the centre of the town, despite warnings of the possible dire consequences of this action'.[30]

Dr Fennell organised two joint protest meetings of Cardiff's black and Arab communities on 13 and 16 June 1919. He said it was the responsibility of the British government to support those who found themselves on the receiving end of racist attacks. In *Black 1919: Riots, Racism and Resistance in Imperial Britain* (2008), Jacqueline Jenkinson says that during the two meetings:

> While forcefully stating the grievances of the racialized minority ethnic populations, Fennell declared his trust in the government to defuse the riotous situation. He hoped that the wider British public would come to recognize the worth of minority ethnic populations. The convening of the meeting in a mission room, Fennell's biblical reference to the origins of black people as the 'descendants of Ham' and his appeal to the Christian tolerance of white society suggest Fennell had acquired a British missionary education.[31]

In *Staying Power* (1984), Peter Fryer describes Dr Fennell as 31 years of age, about 6ft tall, and a well-dressed and highly articulate man who acted as the community's spokesman in negotiations with the authorities:

> [He] pressed the claims of those who wanted to be repatriated; told reporters 'that it is absolutely necessary to grip the evil, and not to play with it'; and told one of several protest meetings held at the docks by West Indians, Somalis, Arabs, Egyptians and 'Portuguese subjects' that it was their duty to stay within the law, but 'if they did not protect their homes after remaining within the law they would be cowards, not men'.[32]

In July 1919 in London, Dr Fennell contacted the Home Office, Colonial Office and several Members of Parliament. He pleaded the case of the seamen who were happy to be repatriated, but he also supported those who had made Cardiff their home and wanted to stay. His lobbying brought him to the attention of the British government and one official described him as a nuisance, 'an obstreperous coloured man from Cardiff'.[33]

Christian Høgsbjerg notes that, while Fennell was in London:

> He met up with members of the Society of African Peoples, a black British civil rights society which had been founded the year before in London by

the black West Indian Felix Eugene Michael Hercules as the Society of Peoples of African Origin, with the *African Telegraph* as its monthly newspaper. In 1919, this group had merged with the African Progress Union to form the new 'Society of African Peoples', of which it seems Fennell was to become a representative.[34]

When Dr Fennell accused the Cardiff police of racism they retaliated by arresting him on a trumped-up charge of fraud. The arrest was made on 19 July 1919 in London while Dr Fennell was still seeking audiences with officials, and on the orders of Cardiff's Chief Constable, David Williams. Peter Fryer notes that, at his court appearance in Cardiff on 22 July, he was accused of obtaining £2 by false pretences from Ahmed Ben Ahmed Demary, a boarding-house master: 'Fennell's solicitor told the court that there was "a great deal at the back of the case" and that "certain men were anxious to keep the accused in prison because of the way he had watched the interests of the coloured men". The magistrate dismissed the charge.'[35] Dr Fennell left Cardiff soon after his arrest, court appearance and acquittal, but in 1919 he showed that he could be a forceful community leader.

In Alan Llwyd's *Black Wales: A History of Black Welsh People* (2005), Dr Glenn Jordan, the Director of the Butetown History and Arts Centre, said that the 1919 riots shaped the identity of Cardiff's black community in an important way: 'I think that one of the things it did was say: "We are a tough people. Don't mess with us, don't step on to our turf; we will protect it, we will defend it." I think that's an important part of the self-concept of Tiger Bay.'[36]

Notes

1. Muriel Burgess, *Shirley: An Appreciation of the Life of Shirley Bassey* (Century, 1998), p. 3.
2. Kenneth Trotman, *Struggles for Black Community: Tiger Bay is My Home* (1983) made for Channel 4 television's *People to People* series, directed by Colin Prescod. Kenneth Trotman died in Cardiff in 1999 at the age of 93.
3. Kenneth Little, *Negroes in Britain: A Study of Race Relations in English Society* (Kegan Paul, Trench, Trubner 1948), p. 54.
4. Paul Thompson, *The Edwardians: The Remaking of British Society* (Weidenfeld and Nicholson, 1975), p. 96.
5. Ibid.
6. Ibid., p. 99.
7. Ibid., p. 100.
8. Ibid., pp. 97–98.

9. Edith Bryan, interviewed by William Raynor, *Radio Times*, 7 November 1974.
10. Jeffrey Green, *Black Edwardians: Black People in Britain 1901–1914* (Frank Cass, 1998), pp. 60–61.
11. Val Wilmer, 'Don Johnson (1911–1994), singer and actor', *Oxford Dictionary of National Biography* (Oxford University Press, 2004).
12. Don Johnson interviewed by Val Wilmer for the National Sound Archive's *Oral History of Jazz in Britain*, quoted in John L. Williams, *Miss Shirley Bassey* (Quercus, 2010), p. 21.
13. Ibid., p. 61.
14. Val Wilmer, 'Joe Deniz (1913–1994), guitarist', *Oxford Dictionary of National Biography* (Oxford University Press, 2004).
15. Jeffrey Green, 'Joe Deniz: A Guitarist from Cardiff', *Keskidee*, Autumn 1986, p. 13.
16. Ibid.
17. Little, p. 56.
18. Ray Costello, *Black Salt: Seafarers of African Descent on British Ships* (Liverpool University Press, 2012), pp. 146–47.
19. Edward Scobie, *Black Britannia: A History of Blacks in Britain* (Johnson Publishing Company, 1972), p. 159.
20. Neil Sinclair, *The Tiger Bay Story* (Butetown History and Arts Project, 1993), pp. 31–32.
21. Beatrice Sinclair (née Headley), *Struggles for Black Community: Tiger Bay is My Home* (1983) made for Channel 4 television's *People to People* series, directed by Colin Prescod. Beatrice Sinclair died in Cardiff in 2001.
22. Ibid.
23. Alan Llwyd, *Black Wales: A History of Black Welsh People* (Hughes/Butetown History and Arts Centre, 2005), p. 93.
24. Beatrice Sinclair (née Headley).
25. Llwyd, p. 99.
26. Nathan 'Joe' Friday, *The Black Man in Britain 1550–1950: 2: Landfall*, BBC2, 22 November 1974.
27. Neil Evans, 'Red Summers', *History Today*, vol. 51 no. 2, February 2001.
28. Llwyd, p. 94.
29. Scobie, p. 157.
30. Christian Høgsbjerg, 'Rufus E. Fennell: A West Indian Literary Pan-Africanist', *Race and Class*, p. 4 (forthcoming).
31. Jacqueline Jenkinson, *Black 1919: Riots, Racism and Resistance in Imperial Britain* (Liverpool University Press, 2008), p. 121.
32. Peter Fryer, *Staying Power: The History of Black People in Britain* (Pluto Press, 1984), pp. 308–09.
33. Jenkinson, p. 121.
34. Høgsbjerg, p. 7.
35. Fryer, pp. 309–10.
36. Glenn Jordan in Alan Llwyd, *Black Wales*, p. 102.

18

LIVERPOOL AND THE MURDER OF CHARLES WOTTEN

By 1700 Liverpool had been transformed from a small fishing port into the country's third most important port. It was a centre for both import and export trade: 'coal, iron, copper, Lancashire fabrics and Yorkshire woollens were exported to Ireland and Europe in exchange for Irish linen, leather and other produce. Spices and other foreign luxuries shipped to Liverpool were re-exported to other English ports.'[1] By the end of the eighteenth century Liverpool had also become one of Europe's greatest ports because of its involvement in the slave trade. Since the abolition of the slave trade in 1807 (with effect from 1 January 1808), there has always been a black presence in Liverpool. In fact, Liverpool's black community is the likeliest candidate for being the oldest in Europe, though black settlements have existed in other seaports such as London and Cardiff for many generations. According to the historian Ray Costello, what sets Liverpool apart from the other seaports is its continuity; 'some black Liverpudlians being able to trace their roots in Liverpool for as many as ten generations'. Ray acknowledges the existence of black communities in other seaports, 'but there have been gaps, communities dying out only to rise again at a later date.'[2] This has not been the case with Liverpool. Costello, who has researched the history of Liverpool's black community, says that 'in the Parish of St James alone some 34 black adults were christened between April 1801 and September 1808 [...] Black people were being born in Liverpool by at least the latter part of the 18th century.'[3]

By 1919 the numbers of black people living in Liverpool had risen to 5,000. They were mostly working class, but there was fierce competition with poor whites for jobs. In 1919 many black Liverpudlians had their employment terminated at local oil mills and sugar refineries because whites refused to work alongside them. In May of that year white rioters began to attack black citizens in the streets, as well as their homes and businesses. The Elder Dempster Shipping Line's hostel for West African sailors and the David Lewis Hostel for black ratings were attacked and many houses in Parliament Street, Chester Street and Stanhope Street were targeted and set alight. *The Times* (11 June 1919) reported that 'the district was in an uproar and every coloured man seen was followed by large hostile crowds'. *The Times* reported that some of the black victims stated that they were British subjects and asked for justice and fair play: 'During the war they obtained employment without difficulty, but with unemployment which has lately come about there has been bitterness shown towards them.'[4] Says Ray Costello:

> The scenes might have prefigured the infamous *Kristallnacht* [or 'night of the broken glass'] in Germany in 1938, when Jewish premises had their windows broken, and many were set on fire. In a climate of widespread unemployment, feelings ran high against black people who, wrongly in the case of the majority of Liverpool blacks, were considered newcomers to these shores.[5]

Grace Wilkie (née Walker) was born in Liverpool in 1918 to Cratue Walker, an African seaman who had married his English wife, Elizabeth Cropper, in Liverpool in 1916. When she was interviewed by Ray Costello, she remembered what her mother had told her, when she was old enough to understand:

> She said that all the whites and the blacks were fighting. There was cutting, some got arrested and she was compelled at that time to put me in a tin bath and cover me over with blankets and planks to protect me, because they were throwing bottles and bricks, and anything – you name it – through the windows.[6]

To shield them from the violence, the local police took many black families to the safety of 'bridewell' (a local gaol) in Argyle Street. On 11 June 1919, Liverpool's *Evening Express* described what happened:

Wrecked houses, despoiled of their furniture, gaping holes in plate glass windows, shops which have been broken open by hooligans and emptied of their contents by thieves, and charred patches in the road to denote the bonfire made by some innocent person's furniture are visible evidence of the result of rioting in the negro colony of Liverpool last night [...] The negroes by the hundred have thrown themselves upon the mercy of the authorities. In dozens they presented themselves at the bridewell yesterday afternoon and evening, and before today's dawn broke there were between 600 and 700 black men safely housed at their own request in the main bridewell at Cheapside. During the day this number has been considerably increased. Four hundred were marched through the streets by the police [...] About 70 black men who were taking refuge in the Ethiopian Hall, Brownlow Hill, were yesterday removed in the prison van, the police fearing that the place would be attacked. This action was a wise one, for it was soon afterwards discovered that there were several large gangs of roughs from the Pitt Street locality hiding in the side streets ready for causing trouble.[7]

The hatred of the white rioters for Liverpool's black community was reported in several newspapers. The 'Liverpool correspondent' for the *Manchester Guardian* described Pitt Street in a news report published on 7 June 1919 as an 'unsavoury neighbourhood near the docks'. However, the tone of the article gave a distorted and misleading image of Liverpool's black citizens, some of whom had served Britain in the war:

For some time now a good deal of bitterness has been shown by the white population of the neighbourhood, who have made complaints about the low moral standard of the blacks, whose consorting with white women has caused much resentment. 'These men,' said a white resident, 'are taking the bread out of the mouths of the discharged soldiers.'

On 12 June a reporter for the *Manchester Guardian* visited Liverpool and interviewed an 'experienced' but nameless police officer who claimed that the people of his city 'understand negroes and make allowance for their vanity and bragging. They know that most of them are only big children who, when they get money, like to make a show, and especially to dress well'.

In November 1919, fifteen black men found themselves on trial for their alleged involvement in the Liverpool riots. They were charged with 'riotous assembly and assault'. Their defence counsel was Edward Theophilus Nelson, a Guyanese lawyer who had studied at St John's College, Oxford from 1898 to 1902. Nelson's fees were paid by the African Progress Union (see Chapter 19), a London-based black civil rights group led by John Archer, the prominent black activist and Labour councillor in Battersea. Says Sam Davies in the *Oxford Dictionary of National Biography*:

> The case against the men was based mainly on identification by police and bystanders, much of which was unreliable and at times contra-dictory, and five of the fifteen accused were acquitted. The other ten, however, received prison sentences of between eight and twenty-two months. Nelson, described variously in press reports as 'a coloured gen-tlemen' and 'a native barrister', was able to cast doubt on much of the evidence presented by the prosecution, and was reported as conducting the defence 'with great clearness and ability' (*Liverpool Daily Post and Mercury*, 8, 10 Nov 1919).[8]

The greatest tragedy of the 1919 riots, and a shameful episode that impacted on Liverpool's black community for generations, was the murder of a black seaman on 5 June 1919. Not much is known about the victim, Charles Wotten, a 24-year-old ship's fireman from Bermuda.[9] After serving his king and country in the First World War, Charles was discharged from the Royal Navy in March 1919. He was lodging at 18 Pitt Street, a boarding house for black seamen in Liverpool's dockland area, when the police raided it. They were responding to a disturbance that had taken place at another address. At the boarding house, a police constable saw Charles, who had escaped from the boarding house, being chased by a large crowd of about 200–300 rioters. The police ran after him, but the crowd chased him to Queen's Dock which was located in the Toxteth area. By the time the police reached him, the crowd were throwing all kinds of missiles at Charles. The crowd forced him into the water where he drowned. Said the *Evening Express* (10 June 1919): 'The police offic-ers, who had hold of him, did their best to protect him from the excited crowd, but the latter succeeded in wrenching him away. Witness could not positively say whether the negro was thrown in the dock or jumped in, or was swept by the swaying crowd.'[10] Ernest Marke (see Chapter 15) recalled the incident in his autobiography *Old Man Trouble* (1975):

'In Liverpool dockside, a negro whom I knew was being chased by a crowd of John Bulls and found himself trapped. He jumped into the river, trying to swim to a ship [...] while he was swimming the crowd hooted and threw bricks at him.'[11]

No arrests were made and the police report states that:

Whilst attempting to take Wootton [*sic*] out of the dock gates, under arrest, the crowd surged forward, overwhelming the Constables, knocking them to the ground. The Constables fought desperately to protect him [...] Wootton was dragged off by the crowd, beaten, weighed down by anchor chain and thrown into the dock and drowned. After this, the Police employed heavy tactics, baton and Mounted Police charges, which dispersed the crowd. Wootton's body was recovered some hours later.[12]

A factor which may have led to Charles's death was the absence of police officers on the streets. The Liverpool police were on strike in 1919 and may not have had the resources to control the crowds or investigate the murder. In Britain 50 per cent of the force went on strike that year and 955 were dismissed.[13] The actions of the crowd, chasing Charles into the water, must have been encouraged by the realisation that the police were restricted in their numbers on that fateful night.

The actions of the crowd on 5 June and the circumstances of the brutal murder of Charles Wotten echoed the Ku Klux Klan's lynching of African-American men. This had recently been depicted in D.W. Griffith's controversial silent film melodrama *The Birth of a Nation* (1915) with the lynching of the slave Gus. Griffith's film glorified America's 'Old South' and slavery and the South's role in the American Civil War of 1861–65. Most objectionable was the film's portrayal of the racist and murderous Ku Klux Klan as heroes. The film's release in the United States was met with protests from organisations such as the NAACP (National Association for the Advancement of Coloured People), other African American groups and their white allies. In Britain Dr John Alcindor, who was elected president of the African Progress Union in 1921, complained to the British Board of Film Censors about Griffith's film. Undoubtedly the film stirred up racial hatred in the United States, and it could be argued that, after the film's London premiere on 27 September 1915, and its popularity with British cinemagoers, it may have increased racial tension and influenced some of the white rioters who attacked Britain's black citizens in 1919.

On 10 June 1919 a delegation of black men visited the office of the *Liverpool Echo* and handed over a statement. They were led by the secretary of the Ethiopian Hall (off Brownlow Hill) where some of them had taken refuge during the riots. It said:

> The majority of Negroes [...] are discharged soldiers and sailors without employment; in fact some of them are practically starving, work having been refused them on account of their colour [...] Some of us have been wounded and lost limbs and eyes fighting for the Empire in which we have the honour to belong [...] We ask for British justice, to be treated as true and loyal sons of Great Britain.

On that same day, at the inquest into Charles Wotten's death, the coroner decreed that the cause of the victim's death was drowning, but added 'how he got into the water the evidence is not sufficient to show'. It was a cover-up that Liverpool's black community never forgot or forgave.

Notes

1. Ian Law and Janet Henfrey, *A History of Race and Racism in Liverpool 1660–1950* (Merseyside Community Relations Council, 1981), p. 1.
2. Ray Costello, *Black Liverpool: The Early History of Britain's Oldest Black Community 1730–1918* (Picton Press, Liverpool, 2001), p. 8.
3. Ray Costello, 'Liverpool', David Dabydeen, John Gilmore and Cecily Jones, editors, *The Oxford Companion to Black British History* (Oxford University Press, 2007), pp. 267–69.
4. 'Black and White at Liverpool – Police Protection for Negroes', *The Times*, 11 June 1919, no. 42123, p. 9.
5. Ibid.
6. Costello, *Black Liverpool*, p. 75.
7. *Evening Express* (Liverpool), 11 June 1919, p. 5.
8. Sam Davies, 'Edward Theophilus Nelson (1874–1940), barrister and local politician', *Oxford Dictionary of National Biography* (Oxford University Press, 2004). See also Jeffrey Green, 'Edward Nelson', *The Oxford Companion to Black British History*, p. 341.
9. A variety of spellings of Wotten's surname have been used in various sources, including 'Wooten' and 'Wootten'. However, his death certificate and contemporary newspapers favour 'Wotten', the spelling I have chosen to use in *Black Poppies*.
10. *Evening Express* (Liverpool), 10 June 1919, p. 3.
11. Ernest Marke, *Old Man Trouble* (Weidenfeld and Nicholson, 1975), p. 31.
12. Thanks to Ray Costello for providing a copy of the police report.
13. Anthony Judge and Gerald W. Reynolds, *The Night the Police Went On Strike* (Weidenfeld and Nicholson, 1968).

19

BLACK BRITAIN, 1919

The brutal murder of Charles Wotten on 5 June 1919 (see Chapter 18) was soon followed by another incident that impacted on Britain's black community. Peter Fryer explained in *Staying Power* (1984):

> For the entire black community in Britain, the final straw came a month after the riots, when it was decided not to allow any black troops to take part in London's victory celebrations: the much-trumpeted Peace March on 19 July 1919 [...] For Britain's black community, 1919 illuminated reality like a flash of lightning.[1]

The ultimate sacrifices of black soldiers and merchant seamen during the First World War, the murder of Charles Wotten, and the anti-black riots in British cities during 1919 remained in the consciousness of an entire generation of black Britons and their brothers and sisters across the British Empire. They knew what their fate would be if they did not continue to fight for equality and justice, and they passed this knowledge on to future generations. It is a struggle that has continued for decades in Britain and the tragic events of 1919 have been echoed time and time again in a country that has a reputation for taking pride in free speech and democracy: in the 1958 Notting Hill anti-black race riots, the 1981 Brixton uprising, the tragic racist murders of Kelso Cochrane (1959) and Stephen Lawrence (1993), and the questionable lawful killing by a police officer of Mark Duggan (2011). It carries on to this day but, in 1918, just a few weeks after the war had ended, it was addressed by John Archer, the former Mayor of Battersea, when he made a speech at the African Progress Union's Inaugural Meeting. He said:

> Our compatriots from Africa, America and the West Indies have been fighting on the fields of France and Flanders against a foreign foe. The people of this country are sadly ignorant with reference to the darker races, and our object is to show to them that we have given up the idea of becoming hewers of wood and drawers of water, that we claim our rightful place within this Empire [...] if we are good enough to be brought to fight the wars of the country we are good enough to receive the benefits of the country [...] One of the objects of this association is to demand – not ask, demand; it will be 'demand' all the time that I am your President. I am not asking for anything, I am out demanding.[2]

The attacks on black Britons in 1919 were mainly concentrated in the working-class communities of the seaports. There is little evidence that middle-class blacks were attacked, or those who lived in predominantly white communities. However, racist attitudes surfaced. Esther Bruce (see Chapter 12) recalled an incident that occurred in Hyde Park at this time. Her father Joseph often accompanied his young daughter to the park where they would take a stroll and visit Speaker's Corner. Esther recalled that her father always made it a special occasion, for they would dress up in their 'Sunday best':

> In the summer Dad wore a white panama hat, a grey suit and black shoes. I wore a white dress, a little white hat and white shoes. Dad and I were walking through Hyde Park when a well-to-do white man passed by, glanced at my Dad, looked back and called out: 'Hi, boy.' Dad took no notice, and we carried on walking. Then this man came up to my Dad, tapped him on the shoulder, and said: 'Boy, I'm talking to you' and told him to leave the park. So my Dad said: 'Who the hell do you think you are? *Where* do you think you are? In India or Africa? When you're in England I'm no boy to you. I'm your equal so don't call me, or any coloured man, "boy" again or else there'll be serious trouble.' Dad had a real good go at him.[3]

In Hyde Park in 1919, Joseph Bruce, a respectable working-class black man, had no intention of bowing down to an upper-class white 'gentleman'. He made a defiant stand for his rights as a British subject.

Esther said that he instilled this feeling in her, and always told her she was as good as everyone else, and not to allow herself to be treated differently. This was common amongst black parents in Britain at this time, especially black fathers of mixed-race children who feared that they would suffer discrimination as a result of their dual heritage. Some of them did. In the early 1930s Esther was sacked from a job at a department store for being 'coloured'. This occurred in the days before we had the Race Relations Acts and the Commission for Racial Equality. It would be a long time before acts of racism were outlawed in Britain. In the meantime, Britain's black community had to fend for themselves, and look out for each other, and the roots of this really began to come together in 1919.

It is generally accepted that the black community in Britain did not really become established until *after* the arrival of the *Empire Windrush* in 1948. Most people believe that the settlement of people from Africa and the Caribbean did not start until *after* the Second World War. However, this is not the case. There have been black settlers in Britain since at least the 1500s. It would appear that there was a significant number of Africans and Caribbeans in Britain in 1919. When the historian Jeffrey Green focussed his attention on London in that year, he claimed:

> By 1919 London's blacks were numerous enough to publish a journal, to be victims of racial riots and to organize a group (the African Progress Union) which expressed opinions to the imperial government on matters relating to people of African descent. There was also an active group of students from Africa and the West Indies, an orchestra and choir from the United States, three medical practitioners of African descent, a sports club, several merchants and businessmen with a base in London, and enough soldiers and sailors to have their own meeting place in Drury Lane. There were also concerts organized by London's blacks and semi-formal gatherings where further contacts could be made. The fact that nearly every element had a link to another suggests that there was a black community in London in 1919.[4]

The two major black journals in Britain in 1919 were the *African Times and Orient Review* (1912–20) and *African Telegraph* (1914–19). The *Review* was 'the first political journal produced by and for black people ever published in Britain'.[5] It was founded in 1912 by the Egyptian-born businessman and activist Dusé Mohamed Ali with the help of the

Sierra Leonean businessman and journalist John Eldred Taylor. There had been a Universal Race Congress held in London in 1911 and this was attended by Gandhi and W.E.B. DuBois. The congress is said to have inspired Ali and Taylor to launch the *Review*, whose offices were situated at 158 Fleet Street in central London. The composer Samuel Coleridge-Taylor (see Chapter 14) and the anti-colonial campaigner Marcus Garvey were among the journal's earliest contributors. In November 1914 Taylor founded the newspaper *African Telegraph* with himself as editor. During the war, Taylor and his paper remained loyal to Britain and the country's foreign policy. However, after the war, it became a 'harsh and vocal critic, particularly as regards the treatment of Africa. Taylor formed the Society of Peoples of African Origin, which, with the *Telegraph* as its official news organ, called for an end to racial discrimination, the promotion of racial unity, and socio-political reforms in the colonies'. Towards the end of 1918 Taylor handed over the editorship to the Trinidadian Felix Hercules and throughout 1919 the *African Telegraph* exposed the racial tensions in Britain with its reports on the race riots.[6]

During the war, the offices of the *Review* doubled as a communal meeting place for many African, West Indian, African American and Asian students and activists who lived in or visited London, and consequently lobbying organisations began to surface in Britain. These included the African Students' Union, founded in 1916 by E. Beoku Betts, a Sierra Leonean law student, and the African Progress Union (APU) in 1918. The membership of the APU included Ali and Taylor and many other professionals and students of African descent, such as the Trinidadian-born doctor, John Alcindor. The APU's constitution was to promote the general welfare of Africans and people of African descent and they did so for over seven years.[7]

The first of the three men who presided over the APU was John Archer and he remained its president until 1921. John, born in Liverpool to a Barbadian father, had been active in municipal affairs in Battersea (south London) where he had been a councillor and then, in 1913–14, the first black mayor in London. In 1919 John joined the African-American leader W.E.B. DuBois in Paris for the Pan-African Congress and in the summer he returned to Liverpool. He called on the deputy Lord Mayor on 16 June to protest about the riots and the forty black men who had been arrested and charged. The men were defended with APU funds, and the APU also paid part of the costs of the defence, at the assizes in November 1919, of fifteen black men (see Chapter 18). Other APU committee members included John Barbour-James, probably its oldest. He was born in British Guiana in 1867 and served as a Post Office official in colonial Gold Coast from 1902 to 1917. He developed links with Kwamina Tandoh, a businessman and spokesman for West African interests. Tandoh was the APU's third chair. Barbour-James had settled his wife and children in west London and his eldest surviving daughter, Muriel, attended APU meetings with her father. The African-American composer Edmund T. Jenkins joined the 1921–22 committee.

Felix Hercules, who took over the editorship of the *African Telegraph* in 1918, had arrived in Britain from Trinidad during the war to study for a degree at London University. In addition to editing the *Telegraph*, Felix became the general secretary of the Society of Peoples of African Origin and associate secretary of the APU. When he spoke at a protest meeting at Hyde Park Corner in 1919 he condemned the race riots. He also wrote to the Colonial Secretary and demanded that black people should be protected from white violence. He also called for an inquiry – which never took place – into the murder of Charles Wotten (see Chapter 18). In the *Telegraph* he condemned the assault by white soldiers on black soldiers who were patients at Liverpool's Belmont Hospital. When it was announced that black troops could not take part in London's Peace March on 19 July, an angry Felix denounced in the *Telegraph* (July–August, 1919) this insult to the men who had:

> Fought with the white man to save the white man's home [...] and the war was won [...] Black men all the world over are asking today: What have we got? What are we going to get out of it all? The answer, in effect, comes clear, convincing, and conclusive: '*Get back to your kennel, you damned dog of a nigger!*'

Also in 1919, Felix visited Jamaica, Trinidad and British Guiana. His dual aim was to investigate conditions in those countries, and to recruit members for the Society. However, in the Caribbean, as in Britain, the police kept a close watch on him. After 1920, Felix moved to New York and disappeared. It is believed that he died in the 1930s.[8]

In 1991, when Jeffrey Green addressed a gathering at the Institute of Commonwealth Studies in London, he said that the men and women of the APU have been underestimated:

They had broad knowledge and considerable experience. To their broad geographical experiences the realities of life were known to them: mayor, school teacher, civil servant, merchant, author, composer, hostess to Chinese delegations, lawyer, sailor, and medical practitioner. They were additionally with family responsibilities, neighbours, professional colleagues, and roots in Britain.[9]

In 1919 there was another significant landmark. In the world of music, the country was introduced to jazz. The history of jazz is often focused on America and New Orleans, but in 1919 the Southern Syncopated Orchestra (SSO) first took London, and then Britain, by storm. The SSO included thirty-five African-American musicians, and they arrived in London for an engagement at the Philharmonic Hall on 4 July. Afterwards the SSO transformed the London club scene and popularised black music in Britain.[10] Another important figure in the world of music was Edmund T. Jenkins. He had arrived in London in 1914 from America with the band from his father's orphanage to entertain at White City's Anglo-American Exposition. Jenkins remained in London during the war years to study at the Royal Academy of Music. He then arranged and conducted at a concert at London's Wigmore Hall in December 1919 when one of his own compositions was included in a programme devoted to the late Samuel Coleridge-Taylor.[11]

One of the black Britons associated with both the SSO and Edmund T. Jenkins was the young contralto Evelyn Dove. Her brother Frank had been decorated for his war service (see Chapter 3). Evelyn was born in London in 1902 and educated at Cheltenham public school. From 1917 she studied singing, piano and elocution at the Royal Academy of Music and, when she graduated in 1919, she was awarded a silver medal. On 8 August 1919 Evelyn took part in a concert organised by the Coterie of Friends and co-hosted by Edmund in honour of an international group of representatives of the colonial race now visiting London. The delegates included men from Sierra Leone, the Gold Coast and Liberia. The event took place at the Albert Rooms, off Tottenham Court Road, and Jenkins himself took part and played Weber's 'Clarinet Concerto in F'. Samuel Coleridge-Taylor's 'Canoe Song' and Jenkins's lullaby 'Baby Mine' was sung by Evelyn. As a contralto Evelyn hoped for a career on the concert platform but the world of musical revue and cabaret was more welcoming.[12]

After the riots, the working-class communities of the seaports were brought even closer together, while the members of the APU found a voice through their organisation. Claude McKay, the Jamaican poet and novelist who travelled extensively, couldn't settle in England for long. From arriving there at the end of 1919 to his departure at the beginning of 1921, he was critical of British colonialism, disliked the climate and found English whites 'a strangely unsympathetic people, as coldly chilling as their English fog'. The dramatist George Bernard Shaw invited Claude to his home, but told the young poet he might be more successful following a career in the boxing ring than writing poetry: 'It must be tragic for a sensitive Negro to be a poet. Why didn't you choose pugilism instead of poetry for a profession?' he demanded. Claude replied that poetry had chosen him.[13] On the positive side, Claude found employment on the radical weekly newspaper *Workers' Dreadnought*, edited by Sylvia Pankhurst. He has been described as the first black socialist to write for a British journal. He also belonged to two clubs, including the one for black soldiers in a Drury Lane basement, provided for them by the British government.[14]

In spite of his unhappiness in England, Claude did seek out and befriend other black people. However, others found themselves cut off from other black people, and the feeling of isolation could be very damaging. Grace Ann Stevenson was a 38-year-old Jamaican who was working as a domestic servant in Ealing, west London when she committed suicide on 8 April 1919. She had been in England for about seventeen years. Unlike Esther Bruce in Fulham, Grace did not have a strong father like Joseph to protect her; neither did she have any contact with the black communities that existed in the seaports. Prior to her death, Grace had experienced some hostility on the streets of West London. Grace's body was found by her employer. She was lying on her bed wearing a wedding dress and 'all the jewellery she possessed', according to newspaper reports. She left a suicide note, and it is heartbreaking:

My name is Grace Ann Matilda Stevenson. I am black, but I didn't make myself, but people look at me and think I have no feeling. I can't bear it any longer [...] I am a lonely broken-hearted girl, and I have no-one in England. I tried to go home but could not do so, I have not enough money. I have just got £25 and some shillings, but what is that? That cannot take me home. I cannot face the world any longer; it is too hard. I have no strength left in me; God Knows.[15]

Grace Ann Stevenson might have had a chance at surviving her ordeal if she had contacted an organisation like the League of Coloured Peoples (LCP), but that did not come into existence for another twelve years. In 1931 the Jamaican-born GP and community leader Dr Harold Moody founded the LCP in Peckham, south-east London with the aim of aiding black people in need of help. Dr Moody started his practice in Peckham at 111 King's Road (now King's Grove) in February 1913. He felt strongly that God had called him to serve the people of south-east London. In the first week his takings amounted to just one pound, but gradually his earnings increased as the people of nearby Peckham and the Old Kent Road grew to know and trust the sympathetic doctor. During the war Dr Moody received letters from a number of black soldiers who were serving king and country. They appealed to him for help and advice when they were confronted with a 'colour bar' both in the army and when they were on leave. His concern for the needs of black people and other people of colour in Britain eventually led to the founding of the LCP.[16]

In July 1919 Dr Moody took his wife and children to Kingston, Jamaica, to visit his parents. Harold had not seen them for eight years and in that time he had married, in 1913, Olive Tranter, a white Englishwoman, and had four children. Two months earlier, on 4 May, Cyril Henriques, a merchant, his wife Edith and their children had travelled *from* Kingston, Jamaica, to London to make a new home for themselves. Pauline Henriques would later recall: 'There were six of us brothers and sisters, but Fernando was my favourite – I absolutely adored him. When our father brought us here in 1919, I was five and Fernando was three. We walked down the gangplank [at Liverpool] hand in hand; and that closeness remained all of our lives.'[17] Pauline later claimed that she was the very first West Indian immigrant ever, 'but', she added:

It's not actually true [...] my family was certainly one of the first that actually came as a complete family. We came because my father had a passion for English education, which he thought was the most wonderful gift he could give his children. So he and my mother decided that they would wait until there were six of us children, when the older ones would be ready for university and the younger ones ready for school, and then we would come. So, we did and settled in a North London suburb.[18]

By the end of 1919 these two middle-class families were happily settled in different parts of London, one in Peckham (south), the other in St John's Wood (north). The sons and daughters of both families would all receive English educations and make their mark in the 'Mother Country'. For example, five of Dr Moody's six children received army or Royal Air Force (RAF) commissions in the Second World War. His son Ronald served in the RAF. His daughter Christine and son Harold both qualified as doctors and, after working for a short period in their father's surgery in Peckham, they joined the Royal Army Medical Corps, and became captain and major respectively. In 1940 Dr Moody's son Charles 'Joe' Moody, on joining the Queen's Own Royal West Kent Regiment, became generally accepted as only the second black officer in the British Army after Walter Tull in 1917. Moody's youngest son, Garth, was a pilot-cadet in the RAF. During the Second World War, Carryl Henriques also enlisted in the Royal Army Medical Corps, became a captain, and served with the 'Desert Rats' in the North African Campaign. In 1939 his brother Fernando was rejected by the RAF, but he decided to defend London in another capacity, and joined the National Fire Service. He remained a fireman for three years, facing constant danger during the London Blitz of 1940–41.[19]

In the 1940s Pauline Henriques worked as an actress and broadcaster, and later became a social worker. In the 1960s she undertook pioneering work for the National Council for the Unmarried Mother and her Child. In 1966 she became Britain's first black woman magistrate and, in 1969, fifty years after she had arrived from Jamaica and walked down that Liverpool gangplank, she was appointed Order of the British Empire (OBE).[20] Her daughter, Gail Critchlow, later described a family holiday in Jamaica, organised for Pauline's 80th birthday in 1994:

> I noticed how many local people seemed to treat Paul with respect. She had such a mixture of authority, dignity, and charisma that people were drawn to talk to her, and with her cultured accent people found her fascinating. If I could have one wish, it would be that Paul had been alive when Barack Obama was elected US president. She would have been absolutely thrilled. I'm sure she would have realised what a very long way the world had come in appreciating the value of black people since she first arrived in Britain.[21]

Notes

1. Peter Fryer, *Staying Power: The History of Black People in Britain* (Pluto Press, 1984), p. 315.
2. A full transcript of John Archer's presidential address to the inaugural meeting of the African Progress Union in 1918, which has been taken from the journal *West Africa*, II/101 (4 January 1919), can be found in Appendix E of Peter Fryer, *Staying Power*, pp. 410–16.
3. Stephen Bourne, interview with Esther Bruce, London, 1989.
4. Jeffrey Green, 'A Black Community? – London, 1919', *Immigrants and Minorities*, vol. 5, no. 1, March 1986, pp. 105–16.
5. Michael Niblett, 'African Times and Orient Review', *The Oxford Companion to Black British History* (Oxford University Press, 2005), p. 18.
6. Niblett, 'African Telegraph', ibid., pp. 17–18.
7. Ionie Benjamin, 'The Pioneers', *The Black Press in Britain* (Trentham Books, 1995), pp. 11–27.
8. David Killingray, 'Felix Hercules', *The Oxford Companion to Black British History* (Oxford University Press, 2005), p. 209. See also Peter Fryer, *Staying Power*, pp. 311–16.
9. Jeffrey Green, 'The African Progress Union of London 1918–1925: A Black Pressure Group', paper presented at the Institute of Commonwealth Studies, London University, Russell Square, London on 5 February 1991, p. 3.
10. Howard Rye, 'Southern Syncopated Orchestra', *The Oxford Companion to Black British History* (Oxford University Press, 2005), p. 462.
11. Jeffrey Green, *Edmund Thornton Jenkins: The Life and Times of an American Black Composer, 1894–1926* (Greenwood Press, 1982).
12. Stephen Bourne, 'Evelyn Dove (1902–1987), singer and actress', *Oxford Dictionary of National Biography* (Oxford University Press, 2004).
13. Claude McKay, *A Long Way From Home* (1937; Pluto Press edition, 1985), p. 61.
14. John Gilmore, 'Claude McKay', *The Oxford Companion to Black British History* (Oxford University Press, 2005), pp. 279–80.
15. Caroline Bressey, 'A Lonely Broken-Hearted Girl', *Around Ealing*, October 2010, p. 27. Thanks to Dr Jonathan Oates, Ealing Borough Archivist and local history librarian for providing information about Grace Ann Stevenson.
16. For further information see Stephen Bourne, *Dr. Harold Moody* (Southwark Council, 2008) and *Mother Country: Britain's Black Community on the Home Front 1939–1945* (The History Press, 2010).
17. Pauline Henriques and Julian Henriques, 'Relative Values', *The Sunday Times Magazine*, 13 September 1998, p. 13.
18. Stephen Bourne, interview with Pauline Henriques in Jim Pines, editor, *Black and White in Colour: Black People in British Television Since 1936* (British Film Institute, 1992), p. 25. See also Stephen Bourne, 'Pauline Henriques (1914–1998), actress and broadcaster', *Oxford Dictionary of National Biography* (Oxford University Press, 2004).
19. Stephen Bourne, 'Fernando Henriques (1916–1976), social anthropologist', *Oxford Dictionary of National Biography* (Oxford University Press, September 2012).
20. Mark Holland, editor, *The Jippi-Jappa Hat Merchant and His Family: A Jamaican Family in Britain* (Oxford: Horsgate, 2014).
21. Ibid., p. 138.

FURTHER READING

Adi, Hakim, *The History of the African and Caribbean Communities in Britain* (Wayland, 1995)

Adi, Hakim, *West Africans in Britain 1900–1960: Nationalism, Pan-Africanism and Communism* (Lawrence and Wishart, 1998)

Anim-Addo, Joan, *Longest Journey: A History of Black Lewisham* (Deptford Forum Publishing, 1995)

Bader, Lilian, *Together: Lilian Bader: Wartime Memoirs of a WAAF 1939–1944* (Imperial War Museum, 1989)

Bell, Geoffrey, *The Other Eastenders: Kamal Chunchie and West Ham's Early Black Community* (Eastside Community Heritage, 2002)

Bloch, Howard, 'Black People in Canning Town and Custom House between the Wars', *Association for the Study of African, Caribbean and Asian Culture and History in Britain*, Newsletter 14 (January 1996)

Bourne, Stephen, *Untold (Mutiny)* (review), *Black Film Bulletin*, vol. 7, issue 3, Autumn 1999

Bourne, Stephen, *Dr. Harold Moody* (Southwark Council, 2008)

Bourne, Stephen, *Mother Country: Britain's Black Community on the Home Front 1939–45* (The History Press, 2010)

Bourne, Stephen, *The Motherland Calls: Britain's Black Servicemen and Women, 1939–45* (The History Press, 2012)

Bousquet, Ben and Douglas, Colin, *West Indian Women at War: British Racism in World War II* (Lawrence and Wishart, 1991)

Costello, Ray, *Black Liverpool: The Early History of Britain's Oldest Black Community 1730–1918* (Liverpool: Picton Press, 2001)

Costello, Ray, *Black Salt: Seafarers of African Descent on British Ships* (Liverpool University Press, 2012)

Dabydeen, David, Gilmore, John and Jones, Cecily (eds), *The Oxford Companion to Black British History* (Oxford University Press, 2007)

File, Nigel and Power, Chris, *Black Settlers in Britain 1555–1958* (Heinemann, 1981)

Fryer, Peter, *Staying Power: The History of Black People in Britain* (Pluto Press, 1984)

Green, Jeffrey, *Black Edwardians: Black People in Britain 1901–1914* (Frank Cass, 1998)

Green, Jeffrey, *The British West Indies Regiment* (2012, unpublished essay)

Green, Jeffrey, Lotz, Rainer E. and Rye, Howard, *Black Europe* (Bear Records, 2013)

Heaton, Louis, 'For King and Country', *The Voice*, 12 November 1983, pp. 16–17

Henfrey, June and Law, Ian, *A History of Race and Racism in Liverpool, 1660–1950* (Merseyside Community Relations Council, 1981)

Høgsbjerg, Christian, 'Rufus E. Fennell: A West Indian Literary Pan-Africanist', *Race and Class* (forthcoming)

Holland, Mark (ed.), *The Jippi-Jappa Hat Merchant and His Family: A Jamaican Family in Britain* (Horsgate, 2014)

Howe, Glenford, *Race, War and Nationalism: A Social History of West Indians in the First World War* (Ian Randle, 2002)

Humphries, Steve, *The Call of the Sea: Britain's Maritime Past 1900–1960* (BBC Books, 1997)

Jarrett-Macauley, Delia, *The Life of Una Marson 1905–65* (Manchester University Press, 1998)

Jenkinson, Jacqueline, 'The 1919 Race Riots in Britain: a Survey', *Under the Imperial Carpet: Essays in Black History 1780–1950*, Rainer Lotz and Ian Pegg (eds) (Rabbit Press, 1986)

Jenkinson, Jacqueline, *Black 1919: Riots, Racism and Resistance in Imperial Britain* (Liverpool University Press, 2008)

Johnston, Sir Harry H., *The Black Man's Part in the War* (Simpkin, Marshall, Hamilton, Kent & Co. Ltd, 1917)

Joseph, C.L., 'The British West Indies Regiment', *Journal of Caribbean History*, vol. 12, May 1971

Killingray, David, 'All the King's Men? Blacks in the British Army in the First World War, 1914–1918', *Under the Imperial Carpet: Essays in Black History 1780–1950*, Rainer Lotz and Ian Pegg (eds) (Rabbit Press, 1986)

Killingray, David, 'African Voices from Two World Wars', *Historical Research*, vol. 74, no. 186, November 2000, pp. 425–43.

Little, Kenneth, *Negroes in Britain: A Study in Racial Relations in English Society* (Kegan Paul, 1948)

Llwyd, Alan, *Black Wales: A History of Black Welsh People* (Hughes/ Butetown History and Arts Centre, 2005)

Lotz, Rainer and Pegg, Ian (eds), *Under the Imperial Carpet: Essays in Black History 1780–1950* (Rabbit Press, 1986)

Lyndon, Dan and Walker, Roger Wade, *Walter Tull: Footballer, Soldier, Hero* (Collins, 2011)

Ministry of Defence, *We Were There* (2002)

Morgan, Michaela, *Walter Tull Scrapbook* (Francis Lincoln Children's Books, 2012)

Phillips, Mike and Phillips, Trevor, *Windrush: The Irresistible Rise of Multi-Racial Britain* (HarperCollins, 1998)

Sandhu, Sukhdev, *London Calling: How Black and Asian Writers Imagined a City* (HarperCollins, 2003)

Schwarz, Bill (ed.), *West Indian Intellectuals in Britain* (Manchester University Press, 2003)

Scobie, Edward, *Black Britannia: A History of Blacks in Britain* (Johnson Publishing Company, 1972)

Sinclair, Neil M.C., *The Tiger Bay Story* (Butetown History and Arts Project, 1993)

Smith, Richard, *Jamaican Volunteers in the First World War: Race, Masculinity and the Development of National Consciousness* (Manchester University Press, 2004)

Smith, Richard, 'West Indians at War', *Caribbean Studies*, vol. 36, no. 1, January–June 2008, pp. 224–31

Vasili, Phil, *Walter Tull, 1888–1918 Officer, Footballer* (Raw Press, 2010)

Vaughan, David A., *Negro Victory: The Life Story of Dr. Harold Moody* (Independent Press, 1950)

West, Peter, 'Rank Outsiders', *The Listener*, 8 November 1990, pp. 9–11

TELEVISION PROGRAMMES VIEWED FOR *BLACK POPPIES*

British film and television dramas and documentaries have barely acknowledged the existence of black servicemen and the black community in Britain during the First World War. The following is a list of some of the handful of dramas and documentaries – shown on BBC and Channel 4 television – that have been viewed for *Black Poppies*. Each of the following programmes are invaluable sources of information.

The Black Man in Britain 1550–1950 (BBC2, 1974). Five-part series exploring the history of black people in Britain. Part 2: Landfall (22 November 1974) looks at the 1919 riots in Cardiff and Liverpool. Credits include Tony Laryea (producer) and Mike Phillips (series adviser) (see Chapters 17 and 18).

People to People: Struggles for the Black Community (Tiger Bay is My Home) (Channel 4, 15 August 1984). Made in Butetown, Cardiff, this documentary, directed by Colin Prescod, reveals that there has been a black community in the area since the 1850s. It includes interviews with some of the survivors of the 1919 race riots (see Chapter 17).

Hear-Say (BBC2, 7 August 1990). Discussion programme with black participants from the two world wars, including Ernest Marke, a merchant seaman in the First World War (see Chapter 15).

Think of England: Touch of the Tar Brush (BBC2, 12 November 1991). Director John Akomfrah follows in the footsteps of J.B. Priestley's classic account of England: *English Journey* (1934). In Liverpool,

Akomfrah takes a personal look at the history of the city's black community (see Chapter 18).

The Nineties (BBC2, 28 March to 16 May 1993). Eight-part oral history series by Steve Humphries about Britons over the age of 90, includes Ernest Marke (see Chapter 15).

Forbidden Britain: Our Secret Past 1900–1960 (Riots) (BBC2, 17 November 1994). Third in a six-part series includes Ernest Marke remembering the 1919 race riots in Liverpool (see Chapters 15 and 18).

Mutiny (Channel 4, 10 October 1999). Made by Illuminations in Association with Sweet Patootee. Written and researched by Tony T. and Rebecca Goldstone at Sweet Patootee. This documentary examines the role of the British West Indies Regiment (BWIR) in the First World War. Interviews with surviving members of the BWIR include Gershom Browne (age 101) and Eugent Clarke (age 106) (see Chapter 5).

Walter's War (BBC4, 9 November 2008). Kwame Kwei-Armah's drama inspired by the life of Walter Tull, the first black officer to lead British troops during the First World War. Starring O.T. Fagbenie as Walter Tull. It was screened as part of the BBC's Ninety Years of Remembrance season (see Chapter 2).

Walter Tull: Forgotten Hero (BBC4, 13 November 2008). Documentary about Walter Tull, the first black officer in the British Army during the First World War. Presented by Nick Bailey. It was screened as part of the BBC's Ninety Years of Remembrance season (see Chapter 2).

The Crimson Field (BBC1, 13 April 2014). Episode two of the drama series set in the First World War included a West Indian soldier at a Red Cross hospital who died from his injuries. This is the first portrayal of a black soldier in a mainstream film or television drama about Britain and the Great War.

ABOUT THE AUTHOR

Stephen Bourne brings great natural scholarship and passion to a largely hidden story. He is highly accessible, accurate, and surprising. You always walk away from his work knowing something that you didn't know, that you didn't even suspect.

Bonnie Greer, playwright and critic

Born in the London Borough of Southwark, Stephen was raised on a housing estate on Peckham Road and left school at the age of 16 with no qualifications. Self-taught, in 1983 he began to learn his craft by writing for black British journals, including the newspaper *The Voice*.

Stephen Bourne's Black British History Timeline

1983:   Programmed *Burning an Illusion* for the National Film Theatre, the first black British film retrospective.

1985:   Film consultant for the Greater London Council's *Paul Robeson* exhibition at the Royal Festival Hall.

1988:   Graduated from the London College of Printing with a Bachelor of Arts Degree in Film and Television

1989–92:   Employed by the British Film Institute/BBC as one of the researchers on *Black and White in Colour*, a groundbreaking project that unearthed the history of race and representation on British television.

1991:   Co-authored his first book, *Aunt Esther's Story*, with his adopted aunt, Esther Bruce (1912–94), a black working-class Londoner, published by Hammersmith and Fulham's Ethnic Communities Oral History Project (ECOHP).

1991:   A founder member of the Black and Asian Studies Association with, amongst others, Marika Sherwood, Dr Hakim Adi, Peter Fryer, Jeffrey Green, David Killingray and Howard Rye.

1992:   Co-researcher on *Black and White in Colour*, a two-part BBC television documentary directed by Isaac Julien.

1992:   Programmed the National Film Theatre's *Black and White in Colour*, the first black British television retrospective.

1993:   First Commission for Racial Equality *Race in the Media* award for BBC Radio 2's *Salutations* series that celebrated black British, African and Caribbean musicians and singers in Britain in the 1930s, 1940s and 1950s.

1994:   Second Commission for Racial Equality *Race in the Media* award for BBC Radio 2's *Black in the West End*, a celebration of black musical theatre in London's West End.

1996:   Programmed *Black on White TV*, the National Film Theatre's second black British television retrospective which included tributes to Norman Beaton and Carmen Munroe.

1998:   Researched and scripted the BBC Radio 2 series *Their Long Voyage Home* for the BBC's *Windrush* season (presented by Sir Trevor MacDonald).

1998:   Programmed the National Film Theatre's film and television retrospective: *Song of Freedom: A Centenary Tribute to Paul Robeson*.

1998:   *Black in the British Frame: The Black Experience in British Film and Television* (first edition published by Cassell) for which he was nominated for *The Voice* Black Community Award for Literature and received a Civic Award from the London Borough of Southwark.

1999:   Began working as a voluntary Independent Adviser to the police in the London borough of Southwark.

2001:   *Sophisticated Lady: A Celebration of Adelaide Hall* published by ECOHP.

2001:   Presented the first of many illustrated talks about black participation in the Second World War at the Imperial War Museum, London.

2001:   *Black in the British Frame* (second edition published by Continuum).

2002:   Metropolitan Police Volunteer Award for advice around critical incidents including the murder of Peckham schoolboy Damilola Taylor.

2004:   Began contributing articles about black Britons to the *Oxford Dictionary of National Biography* (Oxford University Press) and by 2014 had reached forty articles.

2005:   *Elisabeth Welch: Soft Lights and Sweet Music* published by Scarecrow Press.

2005:   *Speak of Me As I Am: The Black Presence in Southwark Since 1600* published by Southwark Council.

2006:   Graduated from De Montfort University in Leicester with a Master of Philosophy Degree.

2007:   Contributed to *The Oxford Companion to Black British History* published by Oxford University Press.

2008:   Curated *Keep Smiling Through: Black Londoners on the Home Front 1939–45*, an exhibition for the Cuming Museum in the London Borough of Southwark.

2008:   Consultant on *From War to Windrush*, an exhibition for the Imperial War Museum, London. This paid tribute to black servicemen and women from the two world wars including several who served in the First World War (Walter Tull, Cyril Blake, William Robinson Clarke and Harold Brown).

2008:   *Dr Harold Moody* published by Southwark Council.

2010:   *Mother Country: Britain's Black Community on the Home Front 1939–45* published by The History Press.

2012:   Third edition of *Aunt Esther's Story* published, revised and retitled *Esther Bruce: A Black London Seamstress: Her Story 1912–1994* by History and Social Action Publications.

2012:   *The Motherland Calls: Britain's Black Servicemen and Women 1939–45* published by The History Press.

2012:   Interviewed for the documentary *Margins to Mainstream: The Story of Black Theatre in Britain*.

2013:   Interviewed for three documentaries: BBC TV's *Swinging into the Blitz (A Culture Show Special)*; the Imperial War Museum's *Whose Remembrance?* and The-Latest.Com's *Divided by Race: United in War and Peace*.

2013:   Nominated for a Southwark Heritage Blue Plaque for
          his work as a community historian of black Britain and
          Southwark Police Independent Adviser. Came second with
          1,025 votes.

For further information go to www.stephenbourne.co.uk

INDEX

If you enjoyed this book, you may also be interested in…

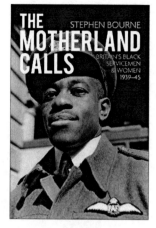

The Motherland Calls: Britain's Black Servicemen & Women, 1939–45

STEPHEN BOURNE

During the Second World War, black volunteers from across the British Empire joined the armed forces and played their part in fighting Nazi Germany and its allies. Drawing on the author's expert knowledge of the subject, and many years of original research, *The Motherland Calls* also includes some rare and previously unpublished photos. Among those remembered are Britain's Lilian Bader, Guyana's Cy Grant, Trinidad's Ulric Cross, Nigeria's Peter Thomas, Sierra Leone's Johnny Smythe and Jamaica's Billy Strachan, Connie Mark and Sam King. *The Motherland Calls* is a long-overdue tribute to some of the black servicemen and women whose contribution to fighting for peace has been overlooked.

978 0 7524 6585 2

As Good As Any Man: Scotland's Black Tommy

JOHN SADLER, ROSIE SERDIVILLE, MORAG MILLER AND ROY LAYCOCK

When the harrowing Great War diaries of one of Britain's first black soldiers were unearthed in a dusty Scottish attic nearly 100 years after they were written, they posed a bit of a mystery. The diary entries were written by one Arthur Roberts while he served with the King's Own Scottish Borderers. They went into great detail about what it was like for him during the First World War. Yet Arthur Roberts was an otherwise unknown man, and little else was known about him. The authors have painstakingly researched Roberts' life history and filled in the gaps. From Robert's birth in Bristol, to his life in Glasgow and time at the front, they provide here much more than just a war memoir, but the unique history of one man's remarkable life.

978 0 7509 5374 0

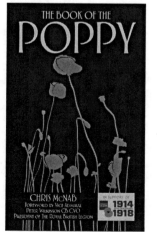

The Book of the Poppy

CHRIS MCNAB

The poppy is Britain's best known commemorative symbol. *The Book of the Poppy* not only explores the history of this unique symbol and the vital work of the Royal British Legion Poppy Appeal, it also reflects on what the poppy has meant to past and present generations. The heart of the book focuses naturally on the Great War dead, symbolised in the blood-red flower. They not only include British casualties, but also those of the Commonwealth nations and of Britain's former enemies, recognising the human tragedies on both sides of the front line. The book moves through World War II to the present day, examining how the poppy remains utterly relevant to the modern conflicts that continue to take lives.

9 780 7509 6049 6

Visit our website and discover thousands of other History Press books.

www.thehistorypress.co.uk

Lightning Source UK Ltd.
Milton Keynes UK
UKOW03f2238140714

235090UK00003B/60/P